CHOOSING
MAGIC

A MEMOIR

KARINA PACIFIC

For Kyra –
Your light and spirit make life magical.

I never saw a wild thing sorry for itself. A bird will fall frozen dead from a bough without ever having felt sorry for itself.

D.H. Lawrence

I aimed to write a story about a fatherless girl, a broken heart and a mother with few answers only to realize God had other plans.

This is indeed that story filled with angels and humanity along the way.

A PICTURE IS WORTH A THOUSAND WORDS

It was a beautiful sunny day in Los Feliz when I decided I had had enough. I wanted answers to lies and secrets hidden in layers of junk and randomness most would consider hoarding. I was searching for clues of my father, of my past, when I found the Holy Grail, "the" picture, a picture filled with a true story yet to be discovered.

The scene is strange, intriguing. It was the first time I laid eyes on him, the missing tile, the one Gloria, my mother, would avoid every conversation about, him, my half, my dad, a handsome one to boot.

The moment I laid eyes on him, I was certain he was the missing link. I held the picture in disbelief of having found gold that could only get better with time. I bet myself over and over, "It's him, it's him, I bet it's him," while fixated on his tall, lanky features similar to my own. The handsome fella was my emptiness, my blood, the one I'd thought about every day of my existence, the one I would have called "Papi."

The day I found the telling image is as vivid as yesterday. It was indeed a beautiful day in Los Feliz.

Gloria and I lived on the basement level with her longtime friend, Mrs. Janice.

I crafted that afternoon well knowing Gloria would be gone. I even saw her board the bus on Los Feliz Blvd to make sure it was safe.

I sat on Gloria's bed facing the pretty garden through the little window next to her bed just in case, perfectly and carefully situated so I could see her coming home, to our room, the room we shared during my high school years.

I had had enough of her secrecy and vagueness about my past when that itch for more truth pained me enough to dig in her layers of hoarding, hiding secrets that belonged to me. I decided the guessing game was over, and since Gloria was never keen on disclosing the truth, it was up to me to dig deep and find answers while rummaging through her pile of stuffed boxes, closet and drawers. The search was the beginning of me and the end of us.

I carefully moved my fingers through every corner on her side of our small basement room. I searched like a starving animal looking for scraps of food, scraps to an empty childhood. And that day, as I made my way through her drawers and looked out the window for her return, I unveiled secrets and scents kept deep in her drawers. I found him hidden between beautiful silk and lace garments, pretty feminine pieces I had never seen her wear. I touched and gently lifted the lace while unraveling the intriguing picture enclosed in a white envelope. I held it and examined his face, his long body, his hands, and interesting clothes...he took my breath away, like love at first sight. He was much like what I had pictured for the last fifteen years.

And after much relief and observation, despair filled the gap I was hoping to fill. The picture did not offer the nourishment I had been searching for and living without, but it did lift the weight from my shoulders, a relief my tense body and heavy soul had unknowingly been carrying. After all these years, I could finally put a face to the mystery man with whom I shared DNA.

Looking at him brought endless light and dark emotions, too much for a young hormonal teenager to handle. So much so, that I forgot to see me.

When I caught my breath, when I finally focused on the burrito wrap in the picture, my cute little face in wonder, bundled up like it was the North Pole, I felt a deeper relief. A surge of compassion for her, for me, rushed through my heart, for the reality I had entered and had been living with.

It was my baptism. Probably a dreamy, sunny beach day, filled with floating, humid coastal scents. I'm certain it was bright, light, and summer like as it typically is in that little Mexican beach town. I wasn't surprised Gloria had covered me in a baptism suit fitting for Iceland. She'd clothe and cover her shadow if she could, and that's what she did to me.

I look perplexed and can only wonder what I was thinking because, when I look closely, I'm alert. I'm alive and kicking.

"I'm hot. Is it winter? Why am I bundled up like a burrito? The womb wasn't this hot. What's going on, what's happening?" I'm certain this was going through my mind while the most angelic baptism gear covered most of my newborn self.

I look aware, while taking it all in through my big brown eyes wondering about every inch surrounding me.

My pragmatic common sense would have said: "Why is she holding me? Why are they staring? Why isn't my father holding me? Don't you see his fist? He's hanging on tight and can't wait to hold me. I want him to hold me. Let him, for God's sake."

And although I am cute, dainty and watchful while listening to a circle of strangers, my fists are also out, out and ready, ready to hold on tight and fight for my life.

SHE'S A GIRL - NOVELAS

One fine day at the OB/GYN office in Redondo Beach. "Congrats!" he said.

I stared at the screen as a new life flashed in front me.

"Hello?" my OB asked with his sweet, gentle voice looking for a response from me.

I returned to the present and looked at him.

"Well, I guess the rhythm method lost its rhythm. I bet she's a girl," I said.

He laughed and responded, "I didn't know people still practiced such an ancient method." He laughed and congratulated me again.

"I'm Catholic, but frankly, it's not about my religion," I countered. "I hate what birth control does to me. It made me crazy, and the concept of a teeny-tiny pill altering my body is something I clearly haven't gotten over; hence, your congrats. So thanks. I bet she's a girl. When can we find out?" I asked.

His focused face showed me that was a lot of information for him to take in, and we both laughed.

"When you're four months, meet me in my office," he said as he nodded, walking away.

Before leaving the sterile office, I was certain she would be a girl and that my life had already changed. I walked from his office as if I already knew her. She would be sassy, smart, healthy and utterly fabulous. I was genuinely excited for her. I was convinced I was going to like her "a lot," and I had a strong feeling she was going to teach me many things. I wasn't sure how in particular, but I knew she was going to shake things up.

I walked out of the building into the world a whole different person. I felt taller while rubbing my flat, hungry belly, and a surge of confidence touched every cell in my body. I loved her already.

Belly carrying was an immensely happy time for me, and I loved that I could make a little human being in a good time in my life. I walked with pride and joy while showing off my belly to anyone who asked. I knew those forty weeks were going to come and go, like a delicious meal when hungry. Every bite of pregnancy would be riveting, short and sweet, and I wanted to enjoy every moment I could because I knew I wouldn't make the same child again.

I felt utterly blessed, and I intended to eat up every second of the work she and I would share.

I imagine motherhood impacts everyone in their own way. Pregnancy for me brought a dose of clarity and a mental decision to get out of my way with all my might. To consciously mother my growing, kicking fetus based on "her" experience, and not on my lack of. To raise her based on her needs and not my fears. I wanted her to have HER happy childhood, a decision I still make every morning I see her sleepy face surrendering to her day. And sometimes a mindful and mental task when one hasn't been mothered herself as a child should be.

Kyra turned 16 this year, and I think we're doing all right.

Growing up with my mother, Gloria, was not particularly the most chipper of times. She did provide food, shelter, good doctors and schools, all of which I never took for granted considering kids around the world who lack some or all of those things.

Gloria struggled as a lonely single mother with slim support from her family in a time and culture where being unmarried with a bastard child was frowned upon in many levels, but she did the best she could.

Her sisters, the ones I called "mean aunties," showed their deep frowns with disdain when they "had" to help Gloria with me. Their angry wrinkles formed valleys down to their necks showing how miserable they were. Their beautiful indigenous Indian features were overshadowed by their grumpiness, features and looks my DNA does not seem to share with them.

Features that often led me to wonder if I was adopted or found on the streets by Gloria. It was a constant reminder that I was not like them.

On the bright side, celebrating my birthday was important to Gloria. A nice dress with a pretty collar, a sweet matching belt, fancy white shoes with socks folded down embellished with lace for a girly touch and a cake. A cake surrounded by kids I didn't know or played with and a picture, only one image to show evidence I was celebrated with a birthday bash, Gloria style.

I've always wondered why just one picture for every birthday. Maybe because Gloria has never been keen on pictures. She also carries the frown gene when a camera faces her and typically covers her face with her hand, like the camera is going to shoot something at her, to which I say, "Relax, why are you scared?" It's a camera, but my common-sense statements were never welcomed by her, which typically deepened her frown.

She doesn't have many pictures of her childhood or mine, so I can't imagine she would have ever owned a camera. I'm convinced she paid someone she once saw taking an image to snap one every year, just one for evidence and fitting for her pocketbook. I'll admit, it was the effort that counted.

Unfortunately, Gloria was not the happiest in the bunch. If I tried, I could probably count how many times I have heard her belly laugh, the kind of laugher that would take years off her life. Sadness, victimhood and fear come to mind, all of which she has carried most of her life while parenting me. Feelings that have weighed her fragile, petite body into sickness, bitterness, tiredness and a mild case of hypochondria. I'm convinced this is why I am so sensitive to those heavy handicapping feelings many carry around for free. Growing up with her burden was too much to take for a young girl.

I never learned why her life carried so many negative emotions, most importantly, why she allowed them to pollute her body. If I had to guess, it could very well be her addiction to telenovelas, Mexican soap operas.

Yes, my people have an affinity for old-school juicy novelas. Novelas that entail illogical story lines, comedic in their ridiculousness and just downright Mexican drama. Every character in a novella backstabs every family member, cheating runs rampant, money deceit divides everyone in the family causing class divisions, leaving one side to eat the bare minimum in a shack with no hot water, while the other lives in ranches with tables full of food, horses and maid service. It's dramatic writing, editing and directing, and people like my mother get suckered in.

The sudden outcries of despair in novelas are the experience of a lifetime.

"Alfredoooooo, porqueeee????"
"Alfredo, whyyyyyy?" Like the character never saw it coming.

Face slaps ruining pretty makeup and sudden, deep apologetic hugs with rivers of tears, endless sorrow and let's not forget one or two characters dropped like a bad habit. Yes, a juicy novela must include death in a story line, more rivers and lakes of tears to be had.

I'm a fan of the saying, "The trend is your friend," and that was her trend. Novelas matched much in her life.

Gloria's family was indeed unfair to her. Their little support was exhibited with distance, and when they did help, they did it with disdain. Unfortunately for me, by no fault of my own, I was the innocent bystander. After all, I was the family's bastard child. Oh yes, novelas also have bastard children roaming around the story line.

Gloria was, however, tenacious, resourceful and eager- and still is. Being the last of nine, and probably a last thought, she was forced to grow up on her own. She never learned to drive, but she could get anyone across any town like it was her destiny.

My mother, Gloria, didn't teach me about this funny thing we do, life. She did teach me that one can rise above deep-seated pain, and that pain should be fuel to rise above any circumstance, even if you're driving alone.

As for me, mothering my child, my precious girl, I can only hope I have served her well while nourishing and encouraging her journey, HER LIFE.

3

AMERICA IS AS DELICIOUS AS BUTTER PECAN

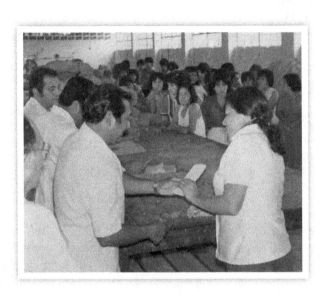

I met Abi two years ago. Her yearning felt familiar. It was at a distant family gathering when we met and were immediately bonded by the blood running through our veins. Her playfulness and gentle spirit were much like a 10-year-old's would be, filled with wonder, curiosity and lightness. The spark in her eyes had me at hello. Her sweet gentleness was disarming, causing everyone around her to immediately feel calm. But if one really looked, her thirst and hopes were as transparent and colorful as coral reefs in Fiji. I saw it in her eyes then and now, two years later. Her demeanor was apparent when her shoulders dropped, reminding herself of her reality, that after this visit in "the land of dreams," she'd have to return to our motherland where life is vanilla, and America is as tasty as butter pecan with sprinkles and stars on top. There is simply no comparison, and only those who have lived it both know it.

Abi's somber eyes said it all: "I am capable of more. I'd like to live in America." And not even the new iPad I had gifted her that afternoon could replace her missing tile, her heart's desire, even though she would be the only 10-year-old owner of a brand-new device in our poor hometown and for miles around. I could feel all of her sentiments, wishes and realizations that America could not be replaced with materialism, that although we would be able to connect with her pretty new gadget, she'd take America any day.

It is those intangible desires of the heart that matter most, the ones that can't be bought, replaced or truly lived.

Wonder and curiosity are a recipe for success I've come to discover, and of course I didn't know this when I was the only child of the only single mother working in the factory. And my not knowing my lack was my gift of survival, then and now.

I've come to realize Gloria was a one of a kind in her time and place. She was the only single mother in her family from what I have been told and from my own memories. My mother worked full-time, owned her own home and depended on no one, much less a man who'd require a cold *cerveza* at the end of the day. She was steadfast and stubborn in her journey, an admirable trait, but one that can be lonely if not careful and open enough to let goodness in.

Young life for me was a mystery of plans. I never knew what she had up her sleeve for me in general, much less when she worked, and when options shut the door in her face, she'd take me to the factory.

During this period, she worked in a tall, skinny, long building where she and others sewed uniforms, endless lines of uniforms.

I spent lots of time waiting for her while quietly sneaking onto sewing machines where I'd mentally escape and pretend to sew the very best garment made in Tampico. Sewing machines were lined on one side in long rows, with cutting tables on the other, like a train. The factory room was high, bright with endless windows for natural light that was very pleasing; it almost felt as one was outdoors. A rhythmic, clicking flow orchestrated by hundreds of sewing machines, pedal clicks and bouncing needles from one side to the other created a gentle symphony. Rows of heads looking down as they maneuvered each cloth, left arm directing the garment being sewn and right hand on the wheel, all creating the perfect stitch line.

The room smelled liked a mix of industrial toxicity only fabrics and threads can emit, and a cloudy cotton fuzz covering the floor filled the room with a day's hard work.

Being an only child forces creativity and curiosity. It means making the best of anything while looking for fun in unusual places. I killed time by sneaking under the long, endless tables covered by layers of cloth ready to be cut while quietly crawling to the back of the skinny building. Curiosity never killed me because it was often that I'd make my quiet journey crawling underneath the tables hoping to get to the very back, the mystery room. Endless legs showed their hard work and age with protruding varicose veins seen through their thick pantyhose and old-lady shoes along my sneaky way as they cut fabric on the table above me with wooden measuring sticks and scissors hitting the floor from time to time.

My quest was to get to the back, the infamous, mysterious end of the building separated by a wall that seemed to cement a division of some sort. For a strange reason not explained to young me, many weren't allowed on the other side. All I knew was Gloria's word to never go back there.

Was it fabric quality?
Were featured designers working in the back room?
Were the seamstresses senior level?

It seemed like a silly division of much of the same, and since Gloria never explained much in our lives, she wasn't about to explain this work matter, but I wanted to trespass, explore and meet fresh blood to smile at and befriend.

That day came when I finally made it through with winning colors. I was as excited as I am now when I visit Sephora, filled with anticipation for all lotions and potions. I took careful time looking around, scoping every inch of the room unveiling the mystery space only a few had authority to see, only to realize what a waste of time I had given this task. It was like entering Sephora with a third of the inventory that I could not touch and no one to help.

The mystery room should have been called "the boring room" with much to be desired.

"Grass is not always greener on the other side of the fence," someone said. Not only was the grass not greener, the aspect of looking forward to a mystery something, the thing that kept me curious and moving, but my mischief also came with a consequence because factory visits became less and less frequent for me after someone told Gloria I was seen in the "boring room."

The factory gifted me an appreciation for work, seeing what women can create when coming together while producing something important. I didn't know what the uniforms were for, and it didn't matter. I relished in the process that began with rolls of textiles, thread, scissors, machines, some pedaling and *ta-da*, layers and layers of wearables handmade by a team coming together to serve one another.

Gloria punished me by bringing me less frequently to the factory, but the lesson was stamped without her knowing. Working was not so bad, that even a seamstress can make a difference. She can clothe someone in the world. That with our hands, mind and precision, we can create marvelous things.

As for Abi, I learned that, even if her journey does not bring her to pretty America, her wonder, curiosity and yearning for better can change the reality she was dealt, we were dealt.

4

A FAMILY AT LAST

Hugo and I were not close cousins until he arrived in Los Angeles in the early 1990s when my then boss hired him in the restaurant I happily managed. Foxy's Restaurant is an old-school classic coffee shop where time stands still resembling a chalet with toasters on each table. Foxy's is where great memories lie and customers become lifelong friends filling empty family gaps for many, including myself. Foxy's is also where Hugo met his wife, the darling and beautiful Ana.

Fate brought Ana, a hardworking waitress, and Hugo together as one to celebrate a bond in marriage, devotion, and new traditions, traits our unorthodox Mexican family lacked in sharing with both Hugo and me. It took a sweet, gorgeous blond to bring us closer together, to bond in ways our family did not practice but all too familiar in Ana's life.

Back home, when Gloria worked endless factory hours and my tagging along was not an option, Gloria's single-mom babysitting options were a mixed bag of locations and personalities, all of which had their pleasant positives and some damaging ones. For much of the time, a dreaded drop-off was Mila's house, Gloria's sister and Hugo's grandmother, the one I called "Mean Auntie" solely based on looks and actions.

Mila and her sister, Gabi, who often visited, were two peas in a pod. Their distinguished, miserly frowned eyes, close-knit small lips, long, straight dresses and hair pulled back with distant stares offered a lot to be desired. By no choice of my own, this was my life for some time.

Mean Auntie time was as fun as going to the dentist, but instead of coming out with fresh, clean pearly whites, it was Mean Auntie's house I'd have to help clean. And when I was done and the season called, cleaning the corn she'd grown in the backyard was added to my childhood to-do list.

I dehusked, cleaned, shaved and then ground each corn ear producing the smoothest, most delicious masa for tamales and tortillas. Every visit entailed cleaning something, and although corn work was strenuous for all involved, particularly a young child, the payoff was immensely gratifying because I could eat what I'd made with my little hands.

When Mean Auntie forgot she was taking care of me, which was often, I played with their handsome German shepherd by following him around the house like the child I was supposed to be, until we both got tired enough to drop on the cold concrete floor, until of course, the day he bit my finger. I don't remember crying; I mainly wondered why a finger was the bite of choice while apologizing to him for pissing him off from all the chasing. I instinctively made it my fault while Gloria added this mishap to her endless list of hurts and fears.

When Mean Auntie truly left me alone, unaware of her responsibility in making sure I was somewhere in the house, I escaped to the living room, sat on the floor and perused the record collection she never touched or played. Every time I swept and passed the vinyl collection, one cover in particular would catch my eye, he caught my eye, a handsome blond fella with bangs.

I'm not certain if it was the rare blond hair because I'd never seen anyone with such a "pretty head of lettuce," the concept of bangs on a good-looking man, or his "look deep into my dreamy eyes" stare. All I know is the first time I placed the needle on his vinyl, any sadness immediately left my body. I floated in a trace of calm with each piano keystroke and note. Richard Clayderman was the man who saved my dreaded visits to Mean Auntie's house and made me forget my missing tile, my father. I played his records over and over and over again escaping into daydreams as I danced my own perfectly choreographed number that started in one end of the house to the other while waving my arms and fingers in the air with the freedom of a child who rarely played, only to return to the cold concrete floor to cool down as the song sadly ended.

Richard Clayderman daydreaming happened almost every time I visited. I played the records so much that they began to skip, skipping enough to break my meditation and emotional escape, realizing my newfound music therapy had come to an end.

One might ask where Mean Auntie was when I played her music endlessly. She did sleep a lot, and I was lucky enough to dodge the bullet for the scratched vinyls. She couldn't have noticed because she never played them. I was convinced they were displayed for looks, to appear worldly and sophisticated. Before me, they were collecting the dust I was dusting off.

When all else failed, I returned to the corn, but for a while I had a storyline of piano strokes in my head to get me through the dreaded Mean Auntie days.

God may not give us what we want, but He always gives what we need. Mila and Gabi were not necessarily the kindest aunties of them all, but on the upside, I had a roof over my head, I learned a little manual labor, and most importantly, blondie, Richard Clayderman, gave me the gift of finding calm and escape in music, a godsend and much-needed musical medicine for my lonely childhood days.

Gloria, in her survival mode, was never aware of the treatment or lack of I received from her sisters until many years later. When she did find out, it only added to the shared bitterness she and her sisters carried. Sibling strife grew into resentment and sadness exhibiting itself in Gloria's life, health and a lack of love from those closest to her.

Hugo, his brother, Effi, and I rarely came together as a family during visits to Mean Auntie's, and when we did, it was not the fairytale Mexican family gatherings I've heard about and seen. I do know that we are blood related, and thanks to another blond, the gorgeous Ana, new and sweet family memories are being made here in America.

5

ROAD TRIPS

"It takes a village to raise a child," that's what they say. I say, "It takes a *caring* village to raise children." But of course, I'm rephrasing based on my childhood and on now raising my teen, Kyra.

When Mean Aunties were not able to care for me when Gloria needed the support of her family, Gloria's best friend, Julia, and her husband, Rodolfo, were the next option. A long distance from our house, but an option nonetheless.

They had a spacious farmhouse with the most perfect front

porch and swing to decorate the perfect all-around family in sight. Their house was on a huge piece of land with fields and long, empty roads, the kind of roads where cars or humans are not seen for miles. Julia and Rodolfo had two sons about my age, 5 and 9, and I was 7 or 8 years old. Freddie, the older son was tall, lean and shy. He had a gentle demeanor and was slow to react; it was apparent his personality was not like most kids his age. His parents never treated him differently, nor did they discuss it with Gloria and me. I didn't care; we're all human with different traits, I thought, so I took him like a brother with no questions asked.

He might have been a little slower than expected, but he had an insatiable gift for hugs and kindness. His sweet and gentle character was infectious; it elicited goodness and overrode whatever condition he might have had. I needed a sibling, and he needed someone to enjoy the simple pleasures of being a kid with, someone he knew and felt safe with. We were a great match.

His brother, Julian, on the other hand, was a rambunctious rascal. He was rough and always up to no good while giving Julia and Rodolfo a run for their money. Julian was always in trouble but intuitive in inventing his own games and shenanigans. He created humor vivid enough to introduce me to my own laughter, laughter I had not found until he came along. Julian's activities were fun and fast, but too loud for Freddie to appreciate. Scaring Freddie into motionless shock was Julian's greatest pleasure and my job to avoid. I wanted the laughter Julian provided, but Freddie's fragile traits were much too important to ignore. Julian was a boy to the core, and I was happy to be Freddie's savior and filter.

Julian and Freddie became one when they saw *E.T. the Extra-Terrestrial* in the movie theater one weekend. They anxiously tried to narrate the entire storyline with love and gentleness they rarely shared. I was riveted as they did their best to convey the plot and expand on the characters, leaving me with a wild imagination wondering what E.T. looked like and why he needed to hide.

A kid's mind can imagine and go wild until the cows come home, until that moment when imagination needs action, so I asked Gloria to take me. I wanted to place the plot the boys shared with the real thing, only to be told "NO."

"¡Quiero ver E.T., por favor!" I said.
"I want to see *E.T.*, please!"

"No, te va a dar miedo... E.T. es un monstruo" Gloria responded. "No, you'll get scared. E.T. is a monster."

Her answer was so absurd that I stopped trying.

"She's probably scared of monsters and placed her fear on me," I thought. She'd never taken me to the movies. I couldn't imagine E.T. being the first after that "NO."

I knew E.T. was not a monster. I knew Freddie and Julian's version of the story was filled with love, friendship and loyalty because after the movie, they exhibited brotherhood in ways they never had. *E.T.* had influenced them that much, but it would be senseless to try and convince Gloria otherwise.

So years later, when *The Karate Kid* came out, and my hormones began to make butterflies when I saw Ralph Macchio in the flyers, I didn't ask. I sneaked out to the movie by myself taking a chance on her long working days because a girl has to do what a girl has to do.

For a while, Julia, Rodolfo and their home became my home during Gloria's many endless working and bus travel hours. I was fed, had a safe place and was preoccupied with the brothers making memories along the farmland. There were tractors and oversized wheels to jump on and off and play hide-and-seek, and Freddie and I pretended to drive a truck that had not moved in decades. Me in the driver's seat and Freddie as the passenger laughing away from our world, mine from an emotionally absent mother and mystery father and Freddie escaping his brother's mischief. Time with Freddie was the most childlike I had as we escaped into our child world and chuckled, gleaning two very different experiences.

Rodolfo had a mechanic workroom next to their house. When the boys were entertaining themselves, which was seldom, I explored the workshop alone while organizing and using screwdrivers and nails pretending to fix the deadbeat truck Freddie and I pretended to use.

Much time was spent doing some of the same, until the day Rodolfo decided to change the course of my playtime, the day he took it upon himself to teach me things, things that would steal my innocence forever.

I have yet to understand how that moment begins when pedophiles decide to become one. The moment they tell themselves it's ok to move onto an innocent being and delight in their innocence and humanity, the moment they escape into the journey to groom their prey. That's what they do, and do it well, and that's what Rodolfo did that day when the house was calm and quiet.

He knew what he was doing; all pedophiles do. They know the vulnerable, the hungry for love and acknowledgement. They groom their victim with patience and craft, with calculating and manipulative words and acts. They do it quietly; they hide while using the shame they have imposed to keep their victim quiet. It's a perfect umbrella for the sick.

I didn't know what a father's love looked like. How could I?

I didn't know was it was, what it entailed and how it exhibited itself. The fathers in my circle worked long days only to return home tired to a cold *cerveza* and little conversation. Affection of any kind was void when growing up.

I would, of course, be perfect textbook pedophile material. I was being raised by an emotionally and physically absent mother and fathered by a mystery man living somewhere in the world not yet claiming his princess child.

Rodolfo began to have his way from the time I was 7 to 9 years old. I thought his actions where fatherly because he was so calm about every step when we were alone. When Gloria picked me up, he was also very calm and poised, like it was normal. He moved ever so peacefully and confidently to convince me his actions were the same he would show his daughter if he had one. I thought it was love. I went along those rides in the open road in his junkie blue pickup truck, and just when I'd relax enough to enjoy the fields, the quiet and beautiful breeze the speed offered, he directed my young soul to his privates and violated my childhood with revolting acts. He was patient and skillful, and once his zipper was down, it was playtime for him.

Pedophiles get into the DNA of their victims, into the missing tiles of their prey's being. They are teachers; they are masters and are not to be taken for granted.

Back home at Rodolfo's, my mother began to worry about the boys maturing around me, and without an explanation or notice, my visits to their home came to a sudden halt. The irony of her obliviousness is that she had the wrong villain in mind. It never occurred to Gloria that it was Rodolfo, the grownup, who'd done the damage, her best friend's husband. Oh, those poor boys.

Life with Gloria was much the same. She did what she did with no explanations; however, this sudden move was perfect timing and required no explanation. God only knows what I would be if Rodolfo had continued to feed his pedophilia, the abuse on my little being. A human being can only take so much, particularly when ripe and young. The abuse came to an end, and I missed Freddie terribly. I hope he's ok.

Rodolfo's sexual abuse opened a can of worms as adults began to expose themselves to me every day like it was normal business. I must have had a sign on my back, "Show me your goods," when my neighbor began to wait for my arrival home to whip out his belongings from his second-floor window or when buying my lollipop at the corner. My neighbor's exhibition was particularly idiotic to me. All I could think was, "You're high enough to be seen by other neighbors, idiot." The first floor offered other exposures of the same creepy kind while hiding behind the wooden fence leaning against the one perfectly missing plank, these types of worms were coming out of the woodwork, and all I could do was shut the door quickly and cover windows with blankets because the curtains were not thick enough to block the sickness.

A couple of decades later in America, when I finally and proudly bought my first car, I began to relish the journey of my newfound freedom on wheels by taking road trips, road trips that began to give me the jitters and unsettle my gut the farther I drove. The more I drove along the flat, dry desert, the more Rodolfo began to show himself as memories settled on the passenger seat while I pictured my young, vulnerable self wondering if he was going to have his way with me again.

It was on the second trip on the 15 FWY on the way to Sin City that I made a jolting decision to not let him take this away from me, too. I sure as hell was not going to let Rodolfo's unkind and demented acts take my love for the open road. I would not give him that power again. So I rode many times to Sin City, Palm Springs and North and SoCal listening to music loud enough to kick Rodolfo to the curb. I chose. I had had enough of him; it was my time.

And as I raise my daughter, my vivacious, gorgeous teen, now getting ready to drive, I reflect on the moms and dads in her life we have been fortunate to have during Kyra's childhood. I think we did ok. She will soon get her first car and create fun memories as she should, with those she chooses to share her life with on America's beautiful open roads.

6

LIFE IS A BOX OF CHOCOLATES

"Life is a like a box of chocolates. You never know what you're going to get," a simple statement with immense truth from the movie *Forrest Gump*.

My family box was filled with complex pickings. Whoever filled my box must have had a sense of humor and an all-knowing plan for my fate.

The older I grew, the more I was left home alone, like a puppy graduating into a grown stay-at-home breed, just old enough to pee in the house and aware enough to feed itself.

I spent much time cleaning our little linear shack, and when I was done with that very fun task, I carefully explored the backyard in search of imaginary treasures, all while avoiding my perverted neighbor who continued his own task to expose his package to me every time he could. This is when I learned to multi-task. "Search for treasures, look away from the perv," I repeated to myself. And when the coast was clear, I sneaked away to take great refuge in our neighbor's house, the grand Mrs. Josephina.

Mrs. Josephina was a dear friend of Gloria's, as most good neighbors are. Mrs. Josephina was older and wise. She had a strong presence and was taller than most people I knew. Her stride was smooth while leaving a trail of silk streams as her dress moved through the breeze left behind her. She spoke with great eloquence and confidence when she shared stories that always ended with laughter.

Her large house sat in front of ours. It was dark and much too big for a woman alone, a woman who had raised a handful of kids, all whom visited every weekend with their own little rugrats.

Mrs. Josephina, her children and grandkids welcomed me like their own. My time with them never felt like they were burdened or tasked. I was made to feel like family, more than Mean Aunties could have done.

When I wasn't in Mrs. Josephina's backyard playing with her grandkids, I snuck into her kitchen to cook anything I could. Her refrigerator and pantry were grand and offered an array of options to cook and improvise, resulting in delicious, as well as disgusting, concoctions. At every try, Mrs. Josephina graciously thanked me with praising compliments after every dish that was edible. The not-so-pleasant ones she gracefully and with great sophistication placed down her fork, wiped her lips, thanked me and excused herself.

I wanted and welcomed any response, any good or bad validation in words. Praise and constructive criticism were rare in my life, void to be exact, so I kept cooking, trying for tastier bites. I wanted a dialogue, and Mrs. Josephina was the first to share it in ways I wanted and needed, constructive criticism.

In addition to looking forward to her feedback after making a mess of her kitchen, it was the kitchen I wanted to be around and admire, unusual and untraditional. The counters were higher than most, and the layout was specially designed for her personality and height. I was thoroughly intrigued by its character and loved admiring each tile that complemented the other and anything around it. It was what one would call "well designed." She had rare and interesting cooking tools I had never seen or used before, and the challenge to put them to use helped my lonesome days when Gloria worked.

During the week, Mrs. Josephina slept a lot, so much that I often wondered if she was alive. Sometimes I began to worry and decided to look away from the pervert neighbor's window and entered her house to check on her.

First, I stopped to admire the kitchen along the hallway and proceeded to her massive bedroom entered through a door that belonged in a church. It was massive.

Her bedroom door was carefully carved through its thick wood, curved at the top, heavy in weight and personality. The darn door was so impressive; it always stopped me in my tracks forgetting why I was there in the first place.

I never found out why she slept so much. I always wondered if it was sadness after her husband died, if sleep was long overdue after raising so many kids and cleaning such a large house or the result of long weekends playing and cooking for her grandkids. I never asked. Any pain she might have been sleeping off would not have been appropriate to share with her young neighbor who liked to make a mess of her kitchen, and although she slept away, I found refuge in having her loving soul ten steps away.

During this nice routine and peaceful time, Lena, an older cousin, began to visit and spend most Saturdays with me when Gloria worked. She lived a couple of bus rides away, which made me curious why the sudden visits since she hadn't spent much time with Gloria or me. But the joy of having family overshadowed my gut feeling until one infamous day.

That day, after establishing comfort as most deceitful individuals do, Lena decided to get friendlier, to explore with my body in ways cousins should never do.

When I said they were coming out of the woodwork, I was not gender specific. They were flocking like flies on honey. I was young and sweet, and they didn't care.

My idea of a cousin visiting would have entailed playing games, jump rope, *Loteria*, and eating delicious *pan dulce* with *chocolatito*, but Lena had other things in mind.

During every visit, she garnered trust, gained affection of a friendlier kind, and as she did that, she began to move herself along my body in ways that would not be common in family unless she took the concept of "kissing cousins" literally, which she did.

Gloria was of course working and oblivious to my cousin's affections, and ironically enough, another cousin saved me in the nick of time and gave me the gift of peace.

Although Gloria never took me to the beach, growing up near it was a treat. Her pride was in being the owner of a house with a guesthouse, which we lived in while she rented the main one. It was easier to get people to the beach, like my cousin, Alberto.

Alberto was a pharmacist. He had an insanely thick mustache, the thickest I have ever seen, like Tom Selleck, and an equally black head of lettuce to match. I actually can't remember ever getting a glimpse of his lips. The mountain of hair over them was so bushy, curly and puffy that it made him look older, and truly, it must have stunk underneath all the hair.

Alberto gave me the gift that keeps on giving, jogging and exercising, a gift that began as necessity to stay in shape during my awkward, chubby years, and a gift that I now use as a means for mental and emotional balance.

On his days off, Alberto picked me up to take me for a workout or jog along the beach.

When I was too grouchy, grumpy or lazy to jog, I begged him to let me simply sit and wait for him while staring at the beautiful calm Gulf.

I then learned to calm my thoughts with the constant movement from the waves coming in and out, each time with a different sound and personality. It became very cathartic and healing to let go of the childhood loneliness and sadness building up inside.

My beach town was so pretty. Soft sand, warm water, coast dressed with beach straw umbrellas and colorful lounge chairs for the taking.

Jogs with Alberto were traditionally rewarded with a delicious cold *Jarrito*, and my flavor of choice was Mandarin. Even when I chose not to jog, he treated me to our bonding day perk.

As if life hadn't given me enough burdens to digest, the inevitable tween years began to rear their ugly head. My body took the shape of Humpty Dumpty, and I never knew what to do with my hair or how to dress. Life was simply beginning to feel pretty pathetic.

Gloria continued to work endlessly, and instead of being shifted around from house to house, she left me home alone more often than a child should be.

This is when my mind began to play tricks on me. I thought about my father more and more.

"When will I meet my father?"
"Why did he leave?"
"What does he look like?"

The questions were endless and always painful.

Sunday was Gloria's day off, a day in the week I would not be left alone and vulnerable, a day God made for rest. We attended the obligatory Sunday mass followed by a long walk to the Mercado, one of my fondest Mexican traditions.

The Mercado is a large outdoor farmers' market. Rows of homemade food vendors to satisfy any foodie are lined up near buckets of colorful flowers to please the eye and traditional handmade gifts of all kinds to empty a week's paycheck. El Mercado outings were always an inspiring escape. The energy fueled me just enough to get me through the monotony of the week to come.

My life box of chocolates began with an array of flavors, many that tasted badly enough to barf, yet it was the good ones that

God handpicked for me to delight in and give me hope. Those are the ones I choose for love and to fuel my life.

7

THANK GOD FOR GOD

Daily conversations with God are a norm. They're part of my days. Praise for daily health, a roof over my head, opportunities to make a living, even praise and thanks for finding that perfect parking spot when Kyra and I are in a rush. Then we call and thank Him and His cool angel named "Kyra's Parking Angel."

She is often asleep when we need her, but once we call on her: "Wake up, Parking Angel, we need you! Where are you, we need a spot!" rarely failing, she wakes up to free the frustration that comes when finding parking in busy Los Angeles.

Some of my favorite times with the man upstairs are during lunchtime mass, what I call a "quickie." Twenty-five minutes of offering the perfect homily, the food for thought, the reason I attend in the first place, and Eucharist sending me into the world making sense of current puzzling circumstances with enough time to grab a quick taco, and back to the office.

Back home in Mexico when Gloria begin to work ungodly early hours of the morning, she would scoop me up from bed barely dressed and half-asleep, dragging me like a doll along the streets to my godparents' house, Margarita and Manuel.

My godparents were the most wonderful examples of loving humans and Christians. They had a lush, beautiful coastal and colorful home close to my Catholic school. My godmother was a beautiful black woman of Colombian or Cuban decent. She had a gentle and happy demeanor pouring words into the world as sweet as sugar, and her skin was thin and soft like silk. My godfather was a tall, handsome distinguished man who always wore a suit, and as intimidating as it was to my young self, he was sweet, well-mannered and extremely kind. Both exhibited joy and love toward each other and everyone who crossed their path, behavior rarely seen in my own family.

Before they were my godparents, they were close acquaintances of Gloria. They were Evangelical Christians, a concept not understood by Gloria being raised a strong Catholic herself, but unlike some of her own family, my godparents exemplified their faith with unquestioned support and loving actions.

It was no secret Gloria struggled as a single mother. What single mother wouldn't? Seeing this compelled them to graciously request the loving responsibility of being my godparents even though they were Christian and we were Catholic. They gave one simple explanation Gloria could understand, "Catholicism and Christianity are God, and God is love and we love Karina."

I would have enjoyed seeing Gloria's perplexed face when their offer came along, considering not one of her own family members came knocking with a similar proposal. I wonder what she thought about the most: the conflict of the non-Catholic section she didn't understand or the relief to have their support and my godparents' Christian daycare at no cost. Unsure of what possibly could have twirled around in Gloria's survivor psyche, she obviously needed them. But I needed them more.

Much of my early school time, after being dragged along the streets of Mexico early in the mornings so Gloria could arrive to work before I needed to be in school, Margarita took pride in fixing my uniform tidy and combing my hair pretty, while my godfather fixed me breakfast to send me off until the next angel picked me up to walk me to school, my Angel, my own personal Nun.

Being picked up and graced to school by the most angelic being on Earth are memories I cherish to this day. I could never believe I was given the prettiest, most angelic individual one has ever seen.

My Angel Nun was immensely fascinating to me, as an albino would be. I was convinced she had come from heaven.

Every dusk morning, she'd make her stop to pick me up, same time, same second. Small morning talk between my godparents and my Angel Nun would be followed by her hand reaching for me to guide me along our way to church school. I held her hand tall and proud. My Angel Nun was the best thing next to tacos. How could I have gotten so lucky? I always wondered. I felt protected, loved and untouchable. I had my Angel Nun next to me and nothing could get me.

Considering her nun uniform left much to my imagination, I often looked for ways to glimpse her pearly skin. Angel Nun was covered from head to toe, so there was little chance of seeing her translucent skin. Her hands and face were all I could see. It drove me nuts. My task was frustrating, but the curiosity kept me busy. Along our walk, I tried to move my hand higher onto her forearm while sneaking a peek; it was my mission during our time together, but sadly...I had little luck.

When Angel Nun spoke, it was as if an actual angel was speaking. Her voice and intention were filled with love, gentleness, purpose and substance, so when she did speak, I listened with all my might and curious soul.

Once at school, Angel Nun walked me to my classroom, and when it was over, she picked me up and guided me to the rectory to help the priest and nuns cook, organize and be helpful.

For many years, this was the routine I looked forward to, a routine filled with loving godparents, an angel, a priest, school, a clean uniform, pretty hair, consistent meals and God, all of which gave me love and faith in humanity, particularly during questionable times. They all exemplified goodness and showed me that two very similar yet different religions can come together for a greater good, to save a fatherless child and help a single mom pacing through life in survival mode.

As joyful as this time was, I could not understand the many layers of clothing my nun and priest wore. I could not make sense of the Catholic tradition they abided by.

Even at that young age, it made sense to me that nuns and priest should be able to have partners, marry and have kids. My experience with them was so human, and human they were. I was certain they needed the loving touch and affection of a partner because that is human nature. How much sweeter would it be if they could marry.

Still, after all the years in Mexico and America kneeling, reciting "Our Fathers," holding hands in prayers and taking Eucharist, I still wonder about the priesthood. I wonder about the hot layers of clothing they have to wear. Is it all really necessary? I wonder about the many locations in the world they minister in, some of which have to be hot and humid enough to forget the rhythm of the Mass. I wonder about their loneliness, the lack of connection with another human being. I wonder about how different their homilies and church would be and sound if they could marry the nuns or another loving human being.

I've looked at my own mother, the life she was orchestrating, the one I was living, and I knew being alone was not appealing. She was suffering without a loving partner. I felt her loneliness and sadness and wondered if that is the way she wanted it, to do it her way, alone, because that's all she knew.

And while considering the alternative of "what if," I still enjoyed the church order because it was the only order I had at the time. As much as I looked forward to Mass, Non-Denominational service made a little more sense to me. The pastors were typically married, speaking from experience while applying black and white scripture in daily life, making it approachable and humanly imperfect. If I had to pick between the two, sipping coffee during Non-Denominational service would be hard to pass up. The Catholic Church must keep up, I was convinced!

Ultimately, when it comes to my sexual abusers, they may have taken my innocence, but they will not take my light, my soul. For that, I thank God because God is love, and love is God. God is not scary, God is good.

8

THE POWER OF LESS

One of my favorite places to be dropped off during Gloria's work weekends was Alicia's house, my older cousin. Alicia was on the shorter side of the family. She was dark, and like her father, my uncle, their indigenous features filled the room with loving smiles shaping their strong features.

Alicia didn't have much; one could consider her poor. And as little as she had, it never kept her from enjoying life and exuding more contentment than most human beings I've met, especially those with more than she possessed. On the other hand, my uncle was tall. He was kind like Alicia, but quiet and always busy holding a cigarette on the left side of his mouth while sipping a cold *cerveza* from the right.

Alicia lived an hour, two buses and a twenty-minute walk on a dirt road away from me. The roads were bare, and backyards in the neighborhood were dirt. The local dedicated soccer field was dirt, and on the dirt we sat to enjoy the games.

Alicia's neighborhood was open land with lots of wide streets and a lot of happy people. They had fun no matter what the day entailed. Neighbors played endless *Loteria* with bottle caps (a traditional Mexican card game), sweaty jump roping on the streets and *pelota* (ball) from one house to the other, finishing off the day with an array of *gorditas* (fried *empanadas*), rice, beans and *pan dulce* (sweet bread), my favorite part of the day.

Alicia's laughter was infectious, even when her husband left her with her two kids. Even then, she chose to be happy with her simple but full life while raising Mariana and Rafa, her young kids.

I loved being in the mix of the neighbors relishing their simple life. It was never about what they didn't have, but about life together. There was always Mariachi, Menudo, Juan Gabriel or Cumbia music in the background coming through Alicia's house from a neighbor who felt it needed to be loud enough to share with the world. Alicia's neighborhood was a great place to be a kid.

On the downside, the nights I slept over, which were often, the early mornings were particularly torturous when the neighborhood rooster stretched its best singing pipes at ungodly early hours next to my window, followed by the neighborhood's *pan dulce* señorita who balanced her large straw basket on her head selling fresh, warm sweet bread for the bite. "Paaaaaaaan, pan dulce," she'd scream repeatedly through the dusty streets. "Paaaaaaaan, pan dulce," she sang loudly with a bit of sorrow, tiredness and skill as she balanced her livelihood on her head.

I always had mixed feelings about this woman who woke and tortured me with her singing as she offered her delicious homemade goods with zero nutritional value. Anytime I actually mustered up the energy to buy her *pan dulce* and eat one, the immediate nutritional deficit and guilt would rise after the first bite. Her *pan dulce* was heavenly; it was a struggle.

In her defense, that was her livelihood, how she earned money and fed her kids, a genuine and simple concept many in Mexico use to survive. She wore a simple dress covered with a detailed embroidered apron. The large, rounded basket was stacked with warm bread covered in hand-embroidered cloth napkins. Her arms fell calmly on either side with grace. To this day, I'm amazed the basket never fell off her head.

The rooster, on the other hand, was just plain obnoxious. *Koo koo ro koo, koo koo ro koo.* He was loud and clear during the same early morning hours. The feathery cock sang with pride as if he knew I was there to get a kick out of it. He passed my window slowly, successful in waking me up, angering me. When I did have enough morning energy, I quietly planned my revenge and threw stones I'd collected the night before. My plan was to push the rooster off Alicia's street, winning the battle of the cock. Leave it to a rooster to make me feel like I didn't belong on his block, but I knew that one day it would end up in someone's plate. I just hoped it wasn't mine.

Restroom needs were an adventure while making my way to the back of Alicia's lot to the wooden shack...let's just say no flushing allowed because there was no flushing of any kind. Nighttime restroom needs were at my own risk while walking through dirt and rocks.

But because there's always good in any struggle, my night journey to release my bladder was illuminated by beautiful bright stars, and fireflies accompanied by a soothing cricket symphony paused at the stream being released from my belly.

Some nights were simply beautiful, beautiful enough to feel God's safety surround me while sharing His earthly sounds, lights and stars. Pretty enough to leave the shack door open to see it all and to illuminate the outhouse. I was never scared. I knew God was with me. I knew I was safe.

Cold showers were a norm, faster and refreshing. Alicia's house did not have hot water, so if I wanted warm water to shower, I needed to heat it and make a mix of the perfect cold/hot balance.

Many weekends when Gloria worked nights, instead of Alicia's house due to transportation issues, my uncle cared for me after work.

He was tall, one of the few with height in the family, and with both our long legs and lanky bodies, we walked my neighborhood until we were tired.

During our walks, he'd grab a six-pack while we strolled through the local greenbelt. It must have been ok to drink in public because it was never an issue. When he didn't have beer in his left hand, he stopped at the same two bars on the opposite side of the street, making me wait outside for a bit. He'd drink a *cerveza* and did what *compadres* with cowboy hats did back home. They leaned over the bar, tired and sharing stories filled with sorrow and surrender from life's happenings. They shared painful stories about *"el jefe"* and reminisced about the day's hard labor with deep empathy for one another, all to end with *"orale, nos vemos."* Their exchange was loud enough for me to hear their stories from outside, which was fine by me. I wanted to know what he enjoyed about his pit stops.

I always wondered why the bars played such loud Cumbia, Salsa and Mariachi music, causing patrons to speak loud enough to exhaust themselves to win over the music. The more *cervezas,* the louder they got and quieter he was when we resumed our walk.

Our walks were long and peaceful in the wide center divider adorned with trees, patting dogs along the way. I pushed him to go farther from time to time, encouraging turns on different streets for different views to explore the neighborhood and admire the homes, always wondering what the lives of those inside were like. It seemed the farther we went, the nicer the neighborhood became, and of course, I wanted to see more and more. I always wanted to explore and expand because once home, it was Gloria's world, not mine.

I got the best of my uncle until his decline began. He began to get slower and older. I'm certain it had a little to do with his daily chain-smoking paired with his Coronas, but I didn't care. He was content and happy. He smiled with a pain only my people can understand as he surrendered to his destiny and space in the world. He never, ever complained.

9

WE ARE THE WORLD

Gloria's factory days ended abruptly, but just as quickly as she lost a job, she found another, a glorified full-time housekeeper and nanny for the rich and stunning. The job paid very well, and I could tag along when not in school anytime I pleased, and once I saw the house and grounds, I was pleased to accompany and help anytime I could.

The Garcias had a traditional Spanish-style compound in a beautiful affluent area in my county, not far from my neighborhood, but a vastly different world from mine. It was class division at its core.

Mr. Garcia was a handsome attorney and distinguished in his manhood and grace, complemented by his elegant wife and equally good-looking magazine-cover children. That was my role, playing with their children.

The house was vastly divided in rooms, pool and nanny quarters and a laundry room larger than my own home. The house had a home feel with touches of luxury throughout bordering on "do not touch" expense.

Quickly I learned that it takes a lot of effort to clean such a large home and that, even though being a housekeeper is an honorable job, I did not want to be one.

Observing my world at a deeper level had become my pastime, my school, and learning that money and big houses do not necessarily make people who live in them happy was a priceless lesson. This sentiment sat deep in my core at the end of each work day when we walked home to our little shack and a bed I'd have to share with Gloria for many years.

Mrs. Garcia was one of the most beautiful Mexican women I had ever seen. She was *novela* magazine worthy. While the handsome Mr. worked endless hours, the Mrs. paced through the compound dressed to the nines, adorned with jewels and beautified with makeup enough to distract you from her joyless stride. Her smile was lost in her thoughts, while his words were used up in trial. They rarely spoke or embraced, but they all looked so incredibly beautiful together.

Spending time in their home, with their peers and their families, was seamless and eye opening, revealing in ways that would serve me the rest of my life.

Even at my young age, I quickly realized that our class difference only divides us by the type of problems we each have and that I would never ever be intimidated by anyone with money or power. We are all human beings with different possessions and different priorities. This is when I was convinced that class division is dictated only by those who need it. Because at the end of the day, we all have to wipe our ass no matter how rich or poor.

The Garcias and I were not divided by monetary class division. We were divided by a joy for life I innately had from a very young age, the same joy for life they couldn't buy with money.

I was 12 when Gloria brought a small black-and-white television for our little house given by the Garcias. A big treat in my world and very much old news to the rest.

It was early 1985 when I was cleaning our little house that Gloria placed the little TV by our entrance door.

After a few weeks of maneuvering the moody antennas for the perfect pixels and sound, I managed to break a flower vase which I swept to the side as a local station introduced a video with immense enthusiasm and consideration for its cause and talent. Distracted by the announcer, I forgot about the broken pieces, anxiously waiting for the video.

The video began with gentle music, different faces than I'd ever seen, colorful voices, hair colors, skin and clothes. Everyone was uniquely different from one another, from my world, and although I didn't understand the lyrics, I was riveted.

I watched intently knowing the video may not play again for some time, and without thinking, I sat. I sat on the broken glass I had placed to the side. I was my own pain in the ass as I managed to insert a piece of glass in my butt cheek. I was in pain and bleeding, but I stood still holding the glass deep in my buttock until the video finished.

"We Are the World" is the cause for the scar in my butt cheek, a memorable stamp, and more importantly, the video that gave me hope.

It was a simple video, but it shook me, woke me up. It opened my eyes to life and inspiration outside my pathetic world. I loved everyone who sang, for how unique they individually were, particularly that one singer with the raspy yearning, powerful voice that caught my eye and ears and the handsome fellow with the dimples conducting every sound with his gentle smile.

Sometime later, Gloria came home with a choice for me, an extremely foreign and rare concept in my life.

"Would you like a *quinceañera* or Disneyland for your 15th birthday?"

Utterly confused by the fact that I was given a choice in my life, and to have "Disneyland" as an option, was hard to digest.

After I grasped the choices and focused on the options and possibilities, I quickly responded before she realized what she had said.

"Disneyland!"

What I was really thinking is, "Get me the fuck out of here, *rapido,* like now." Why in God's name would I want her to work more to save for a *quinceañera,* a traditional coming-of-age wedding-like party, only to invite my family, some of whom weren't particularly fond of us, and dress in a ridiculous white dress? No, thank you. "Please take me to the happiest place on Earth. Take me to America," I pleaded and prayed.

She didn't take me when I was 15. She took me that summer of 1985, and this is when my life began.

10

I LIKE TO LIVE
IN AMERICA!

America, the land of hopes and dreams. Generous America, who feeds other countries, as well as its own. The land where one can try, fail, fail again and reinvent themselves until they get it right. The country with more human rights than its naturalized citizens know what to do with. Oh, pretty America, flawed like the rest of us, you are the one everyone flocks to, and still, they criticize your tremendousness. America, you are tenacious.

I often wonder if I'd feel the same about America had I been born on its land. Would I adore it the same way I do now? I wonder how those who take America for granted would feel if they weren't born into its endless possibilities, into its freedom, the same freedom I see used against it. If they only knew.

The road trip was not one of those quintessential family road trips I've heard of. Trips where everyone tells stories or plays "I Spy."

Our road trip to America was filled with silence and mystery. I remember my stomach being filled with butterfly excitement, my over-the-moon dream-state in anticipation of meeting the mysterious and desired red, white and blue, but I felt defeated by the heat. The bus ride was hot and dusty. The road was plain and long, while I caught only glimpses of sunrise and sunsets, views I used to distract the creeping fearful feeling, a feeling that it was all a dream.

America was taking so long to see. Did it even exist? I wondered.

Why would Gloria give me such a fabulous choice? A *quinceañera* or Disneyland? Can it be true? She's never asked me what I wanted before. Why now?

Just before fear found a comfortable foothold, I kicked it off and turned my frown upside down while making a decision to be patient and stay positive in the heated silence.

Even then, I continued to ask, "Where is this America everyone talks about? There is nothing here. How far is this place? When is the next stop, I have to pee soon."

As usual, Gloria continued her tradition of withholding information or any other communication, any plan or decision that involved me. She avoided explaining herself like the plague, always leaving me in the blind. Gloria could have a gun to her head, trying to force her to communicate or explain why she is doing what she is doing, and sadly, she would not comply. It's not in her.

She went on carrying her sorrows and secrets, making choices I knew nothing about, a trait I have been forced to forgive while surrendering to the journey of my own life with her. And in her secrecy, hard work and resourcefulness, she managed to get us into America legally.

Gloria said, *"Ten, entrega tu certificado de nacimiento, tu identificación y tu pasaporte cuando te pidan tus documentos."*
"Here, hand over your birth certificate, your ID and your passport when they ask you for documents."

And just like that, she got it done.

It was during that road trip while crossing the border, daydreaming and looking at the sky for answers, that I began to realize it was up to me to figure life out, that I needed to suck it up and rise above what I was leaving behind.

We finally arrived in Houston, Texas, a drastic and surreal shift of reality. Where there had been dirt roads and outhouses, now there were endless city lights, high-rises and fast, racing streets I learned to call freeways. As our car shifted from 45 mph to 70-plus, I remember thinking Americans were dangerous and in one big hurry.

After a few weeks of staying with distant family I didn't know I had, we headed to a crowded pocket of Houston. People were spread out on freshly cut grass and surrounded by picnic tables. There were families laughing together. Parents rolled around the grass with little ones, and there was a band for entertainment. The park was lit by rows of light posts, both on the street and in the park, bright enough to hide the stars.

America really is the happiest place on Earth, I thought, while soaking up energy and taking it all in. The scene was better than a candy store until the first startling boom and bang, a continuous volley of noise as fireworks exploded in the night sky. No one told me it was a party for the USA. It was the 4th of July!

I was convinced the fireworks could touch the stars and be seen miles away, while grinning in wonder like a child. I realized the fireworks I grew up seeing, the ones we shot off in the middle of the street, could not hold a candle to this night. These fireworks were the real deal.

That would be the night I fell in love.

During the summer, we moved from one extended family to another, and thankfully for us, we had little to pack and carry along our vagabond travels. Everyone who opened their door during Gloria's uncertainty were kind and hospitable enough, but they were extended family, and like fish, we got old and stinky.

Gloria and I visited other extended family and friends in the outskirts of humid and hot Houston, and just like the last visits, nice to see you but don't forget to write, and off we went.

Temporary hosting carried on for a while, and I of course had no clue what Gloria had planned from day to day. What was once fun and exciting became unsettling and saddening. In spite of it, exploring Houston, bus trips and experiencing the variety of people along the way and the new language America had to offer was my relief, my school of life.

Soon after, Gloria found what she was looking for, a full-time job as housekeeper with The Kinders', a very nice affluent family in the beautiful suburbs of Houston.

The family was a bit of the Brady bunch, a biracial one. Each had a teenage boy from their previous marriage, Ricky and Dan. The boys were as different as salt and pepper, like oil and vinegar. Ricky was prim and proper; Dan was a rascal in every sense of the word.

In addition to being The Kinders'' housekeeper, Gloria became caretaker for their beautiful young girls.

Without a beat, Gloria commenced her duties with The Kinders', and I happily tagged along, never considering what would become of me because it would be presumptuous to believe Gloria's job included her offspring. So, I went along and did what I was learning to do best, enjoy the upside.

I took deep pleasure in walking and biking on the beautifully paved streets the neighborhood had to offer. The Kinders'' suburban neighborhood was tremendously beautiful, exhibiting "neighborhood watch" signs in almost every lush front yard, and the streets were lit enough for kids to play at sundown. It was American living in the suburbs, though I wouldn't know the term until many years later.

A few weeks after settling in her new job, Gloria enlightened me with the news that I'd be returning to Mexico accompanied by a distant family member I had just met. I was used to her not sharing my day-to-day plan; however, this was a different story. I was of course, deeply heartbroken and angry. My sorrow was deep in my belly when looking at her inability to exchange or consider my feelings, even if she meant well. It was this instance in both our lives when I began to emotionally disconnect from her, from her actions and her unreasonable rationale.

And while Gloria thought she had a plan, a miracle would unravel itself without my knowing, one that would change my fate forever. God happened. God intervened and came to my rescue in a bittersweet chain of events when the family I was to return to Mexico with instead left without Gloria's knowing, leaving me behind, a blessing for me and a predicament for my mother.

The woman with secretive and calculating plans was shaken by a twist of fate, my miraculous fate. The true feud details between Gloria and her family are forever a mystery. Bitterness and hurt bring her physical and emotional pain to this day. But that day, it was my destiny and gift to be left behind.

That's what God does. He changes our plans for our good, for miracles. I've learned to orchestrate and plan, always knowing that God may have something else in mind. I mainly promised to always keep Kyra, my sassy offspring, informed and aware of her life happenings. She wouldn't have it any other way. It's not only a different upbringing from my experience, its different parenting altogether.

11

THE KINDERS'

After a few weeks of moving back and forth between strange family, and even stranger family, Gloria's Brady Bunch family, The Kinders', took me in without questions asked. It was as simple as "pass the sugar" for them.

The Kinders' graciously immersed me in their American life like one of their own. Our language gap kept it fun; culture clash made it colorful and, although Gloria and I were technically "the help," there was not one moment when The Kinders' pulled rank. We became as one with their family.

Endless summer day and night bike rides round and round the cul-de-sac with screaming toddlers in the back seat made everyone very happy, even happier when no one got hurt and, although I did not know how to swim, pool time from the sidelines was just as enjoyable on hot humid Houston days.

Just before school began, Mr. Kinder, who spoke limited Spanish, inquired with great care if I played an instrument in Mexico, to which I said: *"Si, la fluta."*

"Yes, the flute," not knowing that flutes are not all created equal when a few days later he approached with a beautiful silver and complicated shiny piece of equipment accompanied by a dark case.

He handed me the case and began to assemble three stunning pieces while discussing that I'd be joining the school band in music class. I was speechless, which was fine considering the lack of English. Even if I spoke the language, I'm convinced I would not have said a word. I froze with grand intimidation by the gorgeous flute, not knowing how to tell Mr. Kinder that I had never seen a flute like that before. I watched intently as he took the beautiful instrument apart and cleaned it with manly grace, while feeling grateful for his attention and the demonstration. He made sure I watched.

"This is how you clean and take care of your flute, Karina."

"Si," I responded in terror. My flute was one simple wooden piece; this flute was a stainless-steel piece of art. I wondered what I had gotten myself into.

It wasn't until the first day of band class that I realized what I was in for, when my blond American music teacher handed me a book with a picture of a flute on the front cover and pretty black characters dancing through the pages inside. I sat in the first seat I found, peeked over the book and covered my thinking, *"Ahi dios mio"*

Panic set in when I caught a glimpse of the instruments lined up in from of me, all of which I had never seen before. Each instrument sat next to a chair along the curved room in front of me. Some were already being held by what seemed to be very confident and ready owners, all my age. The darling American teacher, who did her best with her elementary Spanish, grabbed me to my assigned seat in the middle of the beautiful madness I'd have to keep up with. I could have passed out if she had not walked me to my seat. This would be one of the first I'd quietly rise above, like a pro.

After school at The Kinders',' I took piano classes once a week after Ricky and Dan finished their turn. All settled down just before The Kinders' arrived home from work during my duty of showering the toddlers, just in time for that one crucial thing every kid should experience, family dinnertime, another first for the books.

The practice of exchanging notes about school and the day's happenings while passing the gravy was too foreign for me to digest on the same night, so I stayed curious and watchful while overloaded with information and translating conversations as quickly as they bounced sentences and questions from one to the other.

As the weeks became months, a very pleasant structure that many families consider a routine norm begin to settle into my pleasant future, a healthy taste I began to appreciate.

Fall approached too quickly and, as if The Kinders' had not done enough, Gloria and I were informed we would be flying with them to the South. I was out of my skin excited for flying but defeated to go back home.

It would be weeks later and much internal agony when I realized the South was Savannah, Georgia, not Mexico. I must have lost ten pounds in that time of distress and internal conflict.

Flying was an exciting anticipation for me because it would be my very first flight. I had it all planned out. Gloria would have to absolutely buy me a nice outfit to wear for my first time. This was still a time when flying was a privilege and luxury, even in coach. People were mindful, courteous and respectful. Everyone dressed up and appreciated flight attendants and the experience, a lost appreciation in our time, but not in my heart.

I dressed up in a knee-length skirt with a matching oversized blazer, only to be barfed on by The Kinders" youngest daughter during our plane ride. I was convinced the plane was as close to God as I could possibly get and that it would be impossible for anything to stay afloat without His help.

Back in Houston with The Kinders', I attended an affluent and not so diverse school with the boys. Mainly Caucasian, a few African Americans, and a few of my people. The school grounds felt like a tasty vanilla cake with a few colorful sprinkles on top.

Every morning, Gloria rushed the three of us out the door to catch the all-American yellow bus with other neighborhood kids on the corner. I was often the first ready and the first out the door to grasp the morning silence and cool sunrise while treasuring the street adorned by beautiful homes filled with kids who had no idea what was just south of the border.

Those early mornings were mine for a few minutes until Ricky, Dan and the other kids spilled out screaming from their homes for me to hold the bus. Watching the all-American childhood from the back of the bus, as kids played musical chairs, gossiped, laughed and fought was just a glimpse of the childhood I might have had in Mexico.

Meeting and making friends was brutal and, although girls tried to translate and forge conversations with great effort, it was painfully obvious it was too much work for them. Besides my English as a Second Language (ESL) teacher, who I gravitated to, I spent much of my time practicing my complicated flute and watched the football team and track and field practice while doing my homework on the bleachers. That was my lonesome existence until one day when a handsome African American football player approached me on the bleachers. The moment he spoke Spanish, I knew he'd come for me.

Martin was disarming from the start, and we'd be friends the rest of the school year. Martin often checked up on me enough for me to appreciate what a guy friendship is, even though his kind and thoughtful gestures were much like the brother I never had. There was a comfort of having someone in school look after me. It was a new feeling, and he was a godsend. I knew then God was at work and by my side sending me angels along the way.

By this time, English was beginning to roll off my tongue accompanied by an accent I have to this day. Family dinners continued to be a fun, gifted routine and, now that I was making baby steps in the friend area, family dinners were cutting into my new, exciting friend time.

One day the phone rang and, seeing as I never had a phone in Mexico, answering with my newfound English was exciting.

The main phone was wall mounted with a long spring cord. Ricky answered this time and announced the call was a girl, for me. I sprinted off my chair and stretched the phone cord back to my seat at the table and began my exhilarated tween Spanglish conversation, all the while the entire table observed in silence. Just after my salutations with my new friend, Mrs. Kinder called my name with a stern, disciplinary tone while giving me a grim stare, similar to Gloria's when she tried to discipline me, but Mrs. Kinder's was deeper and meaner with an "I mean business" look.

"Karina, it is rude to talk on the phone during dinner. Please excuse yourself, you will have to call her back." She then looked at Mr. Kinder for support. He nodded and continued eating.

Mrs. Kinder's face went back to her plate, perplexed with my action. I clearly felt she was overreacting as Dan smirked, taking joy in his mother setting me straight, which really meant it was distraction from his shenanigans. It took Gloria a few minutes to realize what was going on while taking the phone from me and hanging it up. She never addressed the evening with me or The Kinders'.

This would be the first of many disciplining and embarrassing moments Mrs. Kinder administered with a particular high- pitched tone switching to a different personality, particularly when Dan was on the receiving end. She was strict and did not make apologies for it.

I often wondered how Gloria felt about someone else disciplining her own child, seeing that she never stood up for me or consoled me afterward. I gathered she was relieved or embarrassed.

Mrs. Kinder's discipline served the boys well. I remember one night during dinner when there was no conversation, only the sound of crickets. I was convinced The Kinders' had had a fight because you couldn't cut the tension with a knife, so I asked:

"What does faggot mean?" in my tween Spanglish accent.

Everyone who understood the word looked up, their eyes popping out of their sockets, except for Gloria, who had no idea what I had asked. Ricky spit the water he was drinking.

Mr. Kinder stared at me with compassion, and Mrs. Kinder lowered her voice while adjusting her expression. She asked:

"Karina, where did you hear that word?"

"Dan, your son. He calls me that word many times. What does it mean?"

Dan jumped out of his seat faster than Speedy Gonzalez, with smoke following his trail and napkin left midway on the ground.

Mrs. Kinder strengthened her pipes, screamed his name and ran after him with a mission in her eyes. "Daaaaaniel!!!!"

Dan didn't make it back out that night and didn't cross my path for a few days. When he did, he apologized and rarely spoke to me thereafter.

Ricky, on the other hand, was kind, preppy and studious. He played several instruments and spoke fluent Spanish. Trouble rarely found him.

The room I shared with Gloria came with a little TV. However, when the family was out and about being a family, I turned on the larger TV in the living room and watched endless MTV videos while folding laundry. Endless Madonna, Cyndi Lauper, Genesis, Queen, The Police, and that guy with the raspy voice I recognized but didn't know from where.

I was thoroughly mesmerized by these videos, and I watched them endlessly while dancing in my head, in the living room, and in the garage while escaping into the music enough for Mr. Kinder to notice my interest in music.

One day, he knocked on my door asking to come in. He

handed me what seemed to be a complex little machine and, considering my last experience with the flute, I was nervous and praying this apparatus was simpler.

"There's a tape inside, Karina, I think you'll like his music." He closed my door and walked away.

I examined the gray box with a cord attached to foam-covered headpieces. The battery was a mystery considering I'd never used them before, leaving me with one option.

"Ricky!!!! Help!!!!" I yelled while inspecting my new gift.

Ricky looked at me with great understanding as I lifted the box to his face. He grabbed it and carried the box to the garage where I'd learn all about batteries.

He took out the tape, read the label, inserted it and said, "He's good, you'll like him."

He placed the foam headpieces carefully on my ears, adding, "This is a Walkman, Karina. Press play."

He pressed the right arrow and there he was, the guy with the raspy voice.

My eyes fixated on the sound and its familiarity enough for me to figure how to stop the tape and take it out immediately. I wanted to see what Ricky read. Bruce Springsteen and The E Street Band's *Born in the USA*.

"Are you ok, Karina?" Ricky asked. I nodded and listened to the entire tape.

This guy is everywhere, I thought. Bruce Springsteen and his E Street Band are everywhere.

Time never passed when listening to Bruce. Music and videos became a translating classroom for me while riveted to each tape. The Police was cool, Madonna seemed mad, Phil Collins sad, Cyndi Lauper loved to have fun, Lionel Ritchie sweet, and more, a perfect array of talent and personalities.

On the weekends, Mr. Kinder and the boys enjoyed watching and attending baseball or basketball games, particularly baseball. These were the days of the Houston Astros—Nolan Ryan aka "The Ryan Express," and the Houston Rockets—Hakeem Olajuwon "The Dream," a great time in Houston sports.

A newfound love for baseball grew after several games in the massive Astrodome with Mr. Kinder and the boys. It was a mix of the serene and beautiful field layout. Its manicured landscape, the wave synchrony, the 7th inning stretch and, of course, those exciting home runs.

On a timely weekend while watching Madonna pretend she was a virgin and helping Gloria fold laundry in the living room, the next video began with a monotonous, repetitive pounding of a pile driver. The sound was empty and loathsome enough to drive anyone crazy, making me wonder where the music had gone. I looked at the screen perplexed as a young man with aviator glasses managed the device with solemnness in his face I could deeply understand. At this point, his face looked familiar while I watched him dust off a base on a baseball field, then he propped up a board, settling into his best pitching position, and reached to a bucket of baseballs, all during the same repetitive pile driver sound. He pitched continuously, offering me the same relief of a baseball game, until the music at the bar scene where he showed himself in a different light. And although it was just a video, it was the quick shift from a reflective works day, to the joy of music and friends at a bar I could understand.

This was the moment I realized the guy with the raspy voice in "We are the World" and the voice on my Walkman tape were the same person, Bruce Springsteen and his E Street Band. It was an immediate joy of discovery and relief to put it all together.

It's interesting what the imagination can do when we don't have the answers and the relief of piecing information together can give the soul.

Instead of trying to figure out the lyrics, I ran straight for my English/Spanish dictionary to realize I was translating a story, a storyline shown through words, lines, and a video.

"Glory Days" would be the first video I'd watch featuring a sport and one that I loved. The first I'd translate on the spot, and the one that would teach me that telling a story about the human spirit through music is an art form mastered by him, The Boss. From this point on, music would become another form to learn the English language and a refuge where I'd make sense of things.

Time moved fast, and life with The Kinders' ended too soon. My imagination went wild figuring out why. I had a gut feeling maybe divorce because there was no way Mrs. Kinder would be ok with the Mr. looking and getting off on the nudie magazines he hid behind the towels I folded. Maybe she said, "No mas." I said, "No mas." That was too many private parts for my young naïve self, fresh from south of the border. And as tradition would have it, little explanation from Gloria was given as we packed up and left.

The Kinders' gave without expecting. They gave with open arms as one of their own, a rare quality and one I didn't take for granted. He was kind and said little, yet he gave enough nuggets to feed me a lifetime. She, on the other hand, was stern, strict and, when she spoke, it was loud and clear, yet she had a heart of gold hidden behind the facade.

Moving from The Kinders' affected me deeply. Feelings of grief and abandonment Gloria could not respond to as she moved onto looking for the next place for survival. The process of moving from one "distant family" to another had become discouraging and taxing, all while still holding hope for the structure The Kinders' had given me.

Unknown to me, Gloria managed to arrange herself in Los Angeles, to rekindle friendships and find work, all while I remained in Houston with distant family, distant family that I actually looked forward to staying with.

The neighborhood was unlike The Kinders'.' It was a rural area deep in Houston. Streets and houses were inconsistent, some with fences or none at all. Their house was strange and choppy, as if they had started with a small house, then added a room on one side, then another on the other side, then a room upstairs with a narrow stairway that twisted along a corner and finally a porch, also added on with steep steps connecting to the ground. This house was so choppy, and the rooms were so odd in size and height, I knew someone was off in their construction plans; nonetheless, I was happy to have a roof over my head.

After a few weeks, my extended family and their teenage girls tried to make me feel at home. I tried, we all tried with little success. It was uncomfortable and awkward roaming around a house with what felt like strangers. I felt alone and confused wondering how The Kinders', complete strangers, could have done it so right, and this family was as natural as a silicone breast—it felt forced and looked awkward. So I just sat back and watched their rhythm and, boy, was that entertaining.

This was the mid-80s, when purple was owned by Prince and obsessed by one of the sisters. She loved Prince so much that

I am convinced she would have licked the ground he walked on. She woke up, breathed, dressed, walked and talked Prince. Her room was purple; every piece in her closet was purple; one wall was entirely Prince and her makeup was purple—so much so, that when I think of her, I see purple.

The other sister loved Madonna and, like her sister, she mimicked her idol. She wore black often, with lace gloves, necklaces that would tangle up when dancing away in the living room.

My stay was not the Kinder experience, but I did learn to watch and learn to let people show themselves, that we don't need to force a connection, but we can learn from each other.

After a few months of observing their family do their life from the sidelines, all I could think of was Gloria's promise not yet fulfilled, the House of Mouse, the happiest place on Earth. So I called her:

"Mami, ¿Cuándo vienes por mí?"
"Mom, when are you picking me up?" I asked.

"Ya es tiempo, ahí te mandaré un boleto de avión?"
"It's time, I'll send you an airplane ticket."

As simple as that, she said little, yet she got things done.

12

CITY OF ANGELS

Onward I went, to the City of Angels, La La Land, the city where my dreams would come true.

I wish I could encapsulate "love at first sight." Those moments, feelings and places when that priceless twinkle touches the soul, forever marking the heart.

I felt that twinkle the moment I set foot in Los Angeles, "City of Angels," the first day I landed in this big, complex, forgiving and messy city. LA is a melting pot of busy angels chasing dreams on busy freeways, crowded buses, narrow bike lanes shared with angry drivers. It is smoggy and complicated, offering an array of cuisine, skin tones, cultures, hills, mountains and oceans to relieve us from the troubles we impose upon ourselves. Yet we stay, we stay because there is no other place like it.

I suppose my love for Los Angeles was nostalgic, a feeling of "home at last," seeing that I was conceived here, an important fact Gloria shared in late 2017 like it was old news. A revealing part of me not freely divulged; that would be uncharacteristic of Gloria.

While eliciting information about my childhood and Javier, my father, who she met here in Los Angeles, I listened carefully while keeping in mind that her stories change according to her mood, the moon or season. Something clicked, and I stopped her in her tracks:

"Mami, espere, me está diciendo que me concibió aquí, en Los Angeles?"
"Mami, wait, are you telling me I was conceived here, in Los Angeles?"

"Sí, ¿por qué?"
"Yes, why?"

And that is Gloria. Why would that little fact be so important?

By the time I arrived from Houston, Gloria had established herself with several jobs and a temporary place to stay while mastering the LA bus system, all too familiar from the time she lived and worked in Los Angeles prior to my existence.

Gloria never learned to drive, so acquainting herself with the local bus transportation in every neighborhood we lived in was a must for our survival. She studied the LA bus system like it was her bible, carrying around rectangular schedule brochures for any bus line we had to connect with. I learned to do the same, quickly establishing my freedom fast approaching.

We learned about the "The Limited," bus lines that skipped two or more stops for speedier routes, some of them connecting through the freeways, a great way to save time, but not so good if you miss a stop or if your stop is halfway in between. We also mastered the commonly used routes and a few private ones for emergencies.

There is liberation in movement of any kind, and to have a wide selection to move across town was an immediate pleasure I found while exploring coastal and inland neighborhoods in Los Angeles. Surveying each community we drove through while eavesdropping and observing every character who popped in and out of each bus was a priceless human education for the taking.

I watched hard-working souls going to and from work entering and exiting the bus, some listening to Walkmans like mine, others listening to mini-radios with little antennas next to their ears. I smirked at the moms who dragged their kids by the forearm like they were rubber dolls. It was familiar. I shared seats and bumped elbows with LA's labor force and could smell them. The gardener smelled like grass; the dishwasher reeked of Comet; the janitor's latex glove scent accompanied the pair falling out of his back pocket and then you'd have a bunch of Glorias too, traveling bus to bus, cleaning houses and relieved when a seat was available for the taking.

I saw pain and struggle in every route, but I mainly saw pride and gratitude, or maybe that was me. Gratitude for the very basics Los Angeles offers. For paying and available labor jobs most will not do, for paved roads, traffic order, inexpensive transportation and that lovely thing called "opportunity."

Soon after, I discovered *The Thomas Guide* and studied every page, grid, street and neighborhood like it was my bible. Gloria knew bus numbers, schedules and stops. I wanted to know streets and shortcuts since I knew deep in my heart Gloria's mothering was coming to an end. Having spent these last teen years as her daughter, I knew she was almost done with what she had to offer as my mother. I knew I'd surpass her ability to mother me in no time, and I needed to be ready for that moment. I knew my life would look nothing like hers, and our time together was coming to an end very soon.

13

EAST LA

For now, I knew Los Angeles would be my home for a long time. I realized I'd have to stay positive, curious, alert and prepare, prepare to make my way in this transient city everyone flocks to for dream and hope making. I knew I'd be ok no matter what.

My first Los Angeles journey was in the community of East LA appropriately so, with an old friend of Gloria's. A drastic change from The Kinders',' surrounded by freeways, the 10, 60 and 710.

A few days after settling in East LA, I began to feel a heavy load settle in my being as the shifting around begin to build up inside. I had gone from a quiet and humbled sheltered life in Mexico to a sudden road trip to America, then emerged into an affluent English-speaking community with The Kinders', to being dumped into a modest Houston suburban neighborhood with strangers, to crossing state lines arriving in East LA, all in less than two years. It would be fair to say this was a recipe to send anyone over the edge, but for now I went along for the ride as it quietly began to boil inside.

And just like that, Gloria got things done again, with no heads-up. I was immediately enrolled into the local East LA school that was predominantly Latino. The shift occurred so quickly that, on the first day, I didn't even have a backpack. Kids at the school were interestingly different, nice, but different. They spoke Spanish, but something was off, and I could not pinpoint it or familiarize myself with them. It felt like being a foreigner within my own kind. So I again, became a wallflower and observed the unfamiliarity in hopes of identifying the issue.

One day, from the corner of my eye, I noticed stares and eyes fixated on me by a group of intimidating students with bandanas and tattoos who approached me with conviction in their eyes, only to offer me an open invitation to sit in their lunch group while graciously taking me under their wing. I don't know what they saw in me, maybe a lonely, scared light-skinned girl scoping the scene, walking through halls looking for classrooms like a lost dog, or the "help" look in my eyes. Whatever it was, they brought me not as one in their group, but one to protect when other mean girls would create an intimidating circle around me, quickly broken by my group, my unfamiliar familiar protectors. I was however not included in their after-school shenanigans, like the "end of day" break they took in the far back corner of the school, returning to hug me goodbye with a scent exuding from their garb that gave me a high if I took a breath deep enough. I was also not included in the drinking and whatever else they talked about in secrecy and privacy. That was fine by me.

The group could have easily been portrayed as the stereotype gang in movies by the way they dressed, by their intricate tattoos or their rough and tough demeanor, yet under it all were kind, funny, sassy, giving and extremely creative individuals.

I loved being part of their group, and even more excited when I realized they were ultimately good human beings hiding behind a rough façade portraying fear and intimidation. Their actions taught me to always try to help the underdog and never judge a book by its cover. They were the result of their environment trying to make their way in their town, East LA.

I was thrilled that they spoke my native language. They were my people, but still there was something I couldn't relate to. The Spanish lingo they spoke was not what I grew up with. The rhythm was longer, and references were foreign as if it was a different culture within the same. I knew the Mexican culture varied from region to region, state to state, but this was different.

Months later after infusing myself into their colorful world, I learned about the flavorful Chicano culture, a chosen identity of Mexican Americans in the USA. That is when I realized what my group of friends had adopted and the reason for the unfamiliarity I felt. This is when it all made sense to me. The power of knowledge can relieve the smallest of matters.

Knowing Gloria and I still did not have a stable home, and unavoidable moves were inevitable, making strong friends at any school was useless, a simple waste of time. Making friends would only add to my pain as we passed through towns until Gloria found the next stop to get us by. East LA was short-lived, yet I found the Chicano culture to be a beautiful, loyal, rich and mysterious, creative and expressive culture seen with my bystander eyes.

During our time living in the small, loud and full-of-love house in East LA, Gloria's friend, Felicia, the grandmother and matriarch of the house, ran the household like a ship. Everyone knew their space and duties, but not when it came to Lucia, her beautiful granddaughter who had leukemia.

While not knowing what leukemia was or how serious her stage was, and why Lucia was always tired, puffy and fragile, I did notice that after spending lengthy time playing dolls, cards and *Loteria* with her, her spirits seemed to lift with bigger smiles, more playfulness and simply being a kid her age. I thrived on lifting her spirits, counteracting the tiredness her body carried, so I offered to accompany her to hospital visits anytime she wanted me to.

The drive to the hospital was spent giggling and playing "I Spy" and lifting each other's childishness before going into the long halls of the hospital. After a few visits, and when Lucia was in treatment, I waited in the hospital's version of a playroom, soon realizing other cancer kids flocked to me to play. We created pretend characters riding along the play train as I used my broken English distracting the kids from their reality. Illness, nationality, language or class were non-existent. There was no judgment of any kind in that room. Everyone had one goal and thing in common; we wanted to play and be kids.

We read to each other and played sweet, gentle games to escape our individual sorrow. Our language gap rarely mattered. What mattered was the time we spent together being kids and coloring our story through crayons revealing our emotions in the colors we chose and touching each other's hearts with a smile, the company and acknowledgement that we have a fundamental right to be a kid, but we couldn't. My innocence was stolen, and they were handcuffed by their illness.

I always wondered why Lucia looked bloated or other kids didn't have hair...no one ever explained. I simply thought every kid was a little sick, and home was just around the corner after the doctor's orders. Lucky for Lucia, she did not have to sleep endless nights like the other cancer kids, but I still felt her sadness, their sadness as they grieved a portion of their childhood in the sterile walls of the hospital, their second home. Some kids like Lucia had the luxury of going home, others to heaven, and seeing sobbing families receive the news are scenes I will not forget.

Lucia was a fighter. She never complained while mustering the energy to exercise her right to be a kid with her tiresome, debilitating cancer. She taught me obstacles are only that when we allow them to be. She taught me to always play, laugh and enjoy as much as you can, even if you're a little tired, and that health is not to be taken for granted.

After months at Felicia's house, Gloria and I began to smell like fish again. Felicia and family were not rude or obvious; it was displayed by those little instances when a family wants to be a family on lazy Sunday afternoons, and as usual, Gloria informed me to pack the morning of. So there we go again. A couple of heavy briefcases carried through the streets of East LA into crowded buses connecting us to West Hollywood because both neighborhoods are one and the same.

14

WEHO AT LAST

There are words in the English language I've learned to love more than others because of their meaning, the mix of syllables or because of how they roll off my tongue. In this case, *agile* comes to mind. What a wonderful word and a great way to be.

Moving to West Hollywood was a drastic change of pace from the predominantly Latino East LA. West Hollywood was mainly Caucasian, where I continued to upgrade my English language skills. This was a time before West Hollywood was cool, crowded and named "WeHo" for short.

The extreme lifestyle and cultural changes since I had left Mexico had forced me to be agile and flexible in the back and forth of my environments. Surroundings I had to learn to adapt to quickly enough to make the next move, a talent that would serve me well for the rest of my life.

Mr. and Mrs. Hundley were our next hosts in West Hollywood. They lived in the area of Doheny, Robertson and Santa Monica, a short walk from the Troubadour.

I always wondered why the big line at the Troubadour when I took long walks through the neighborhood, until years later when I was an attendant waiting in line myself looking over the neighborhood I once lived in with fond memories.

When living in West Hollywood, I learned how Gloria had met the various hosts making room for us in America. Our stay in WeHo brought me a few answers to hold and appreciate to this day.

The Hundleys were a uniquely interesting couple. Mrs. Hundley was tall, broad shouldered and spoke with a deep yet elegant voice. Her thin, amber hair was typically pulled back or very neatly styled away from her gentle face. She wore long, intricate and colorful Indian Kurtis dresses never showing her curves, or much of her skin for that matter. She was an artist. The moment I realized she had a special art studio people flocked to on the fascinating stretch of La Cienega, I became obnoxiously determined and readily available to accompany her everytime I could. Not knowing exactly how I could possibly help did not concern me. I knew I would figure something out with the hope of learning from her and exploring West Hollywood's art and museum display windows I had seen along the way. I was certain it would be more adventurous than sitting in the house alone while Gloria worked as she typically did.

Mrs. Hundley had an array of beautiful, exotic paintings, heavy and unique mirrors with splendid frames, fine Moroccan artifacts, Indian fabrics of all sorts and details, unfinished decorative and chic projects on the ground and the most mesmerizing tile patterns for the picking. The eye candy muted me for quite some time as I took it all in while feeling textures, smelling materials and organizing categories.

I never asked what she actually did with it all, or how it made money, but I can only presume she was an interior designer or art dealer of some kind. What I do know and still visualize is the fluidity with which she walked through her life at home and the art studio. She exuded confidence with conviction through her every day. She approached anything she did with a deep sense of credibility as she explained each piece and its story to her visitors. She covered every piece with grace and a witty story told with her hollow and riveting laughter. Her passion for her world was not like any I had ever seen.

Many perfectly dressed and sophisticated friends and clients visited the studio to discuss items lying throughout. Art and people went in and out of the studio all day.

Not asking more questions is a great regret of mine. I could have learned so much about her wonderful, exciting art world, but I did watch and listen intently, catching as much as I could with my broken English. Mrs. Hundley's sophisticated vocabulary involved unknown art dialogue to my ears. It was too fast and too much to retain at once, but I tried with my curious eyes and focused ears.

I was able to soak up all the stunning colors, décor, richness, art and interesting WeHo crowd, its location and growing culture. To this day, walking West Hollywood, its galleries and chicness, is still one of my favorite Angeleno things to do, one I'll forever be grateful to Mrs. Hundley for.

Mr. Hundley was Indian. He was also tall, lanky and with very fine features. He was intelligent and quiet while gracing his West Hollywood house with a gentle Buddha-like spirit only uttering dialogue offering substance and meaning.

The first time I met him, he shook my hand.

"Nice to meet you, Karina," he said while not rolling his 'r.'

Then he followed with:

"Karina, learn a word a week. Grow your vocabulary." He smiled and walked away.

I stood in deep thought as he walked away, wondering if this is what people do in West Hollywood, or people who wear Indian Kurtis, because I had never encountered such an introduction. I was raised to offer a glass of water followed by, "Are you hungry?" anytime people entered my house.

To his credit, he did follow through with his suggestion by nailing a chalkboard to a wall in the kitchen next to the colorful counter tile recently installed. He began to write a word a week for us to communicate, not discuss, but have as a mutual understanding. Not Mrs. Hundley, Gloria or the others in the house knew about our chalkboard dialogue. I never saw him erase and write the word of his choosing, but I began to follow his weekly pattern. He said little, if anything at all, but the chalkboard was more than enough for me. I was smitten. His care felt familiar, like Mr. Kinder's.

He picked weekly words while his wife overloaded me with art candy. It was so much fun.

I began to realize that each person who had crossed my path thus far was not sheer coincidence. They were not bystanders or randomness offering up casual humanity, protection and graciousness in vain; they were angels and heroes placed along my path just perfectly so. I knew it was God's work. I knew He had my back, so I continued to open my arms for more of His goodness while saying "thank you" and carried on with the adventure.

The first time Mr. Hundley wrote a word for me to investigate on our special board was challenging since I had unknowingly left my dictionary at The Kinders'.' I had one option, to patiently search through the tall built-in bookcase that went from the end of the living room to the other end of the dining room, every inch filled to the brim. It was a collection unlike I had ever seen in a house, and one perfectly designed and pleasing to the eye.

I searched through the book collection and found a handful of dictionaries, making me wonder why a household needed more than one. I looked up the first word he assigned, "navigate," in several of his dictionaries, realizing exactly why it is important to look up a word in different versions of dictionaries.

I was deep in thought, holding several books on my lap comparing the variations of this meaningful word when Gloria startled me.

"¿Qué estás haciendo?"
"What are you doing?" With a contemptuous look in her eyes.

I didn't answer. I stared at her, trying not to forget the various word definitions I was trying to lock in my brain. Her approach was not inviting enough to explain myself, so I went back to my research and returned the books where they belonged. After that, Gloria went about her business, never interrupting my dictionary sessions again.

At Mrs. Hundley's workshop, I observed everything, including her friends' and clients' distinctive gestures. They were pristine and respectful to one another. They greeted with a kiss on each cheek, not quite touching skin. They displayed a fancy, yet genuine hug and dressed in beautiful clothes and wraps. Home and studio time with the Hundleys was always spellbinding. She owned her space in every sense of the word.

While living in West Hollywood with the Hundleys, I slept in a small room I shared with Gloria. I was so happy and preoccupied with Mrs. Hundley's workshop duties, my word of the week and exploring WeHo on foot, that sleeping in the same bed with Gloria was not important enough to care.

Our room was located next to my super-nice cousin, Manni. She was the sweetest of them all. She was kind, patient and a giver, a rarity from the rest of Gloria's crew back home. Manni was dainty, petite, much older than I and a busy hair stylist in a small salon in Beverly Hills. I rarely saw her because she worked endless day, night and weekend hours. She took the work as it came with a smile and gratitude in her face. The beauty about her was not her sweetness or her hard work, but that she was always doing for others. Her hard-earned money was not for herself; it was sent to Mexico for the house she was building for her siblings. But that was peanuts compared to the influence she had in the lives of her siblings, as well as my own.

Many years later, I discovered Manni was singularly instrumental in assisting Gloria and me, as well as many extended family members who entered America legally. She had selflessly positioned herself as the go-to person for legal resources and employment options. And if this was not enough, once those she assisted arrived in the states with a visa, she facilitated temporary hosting and work while initiating the application process to become a permanent resident alien. The rest was up to each individual to create a life in the USA and thrive.

I had navigated through life in the dark, while Gloria worked endlessly to pay our legalization. She did this with little explanation, a great deal of pride and hard work.

Manni carried the burden of changing lives with a smile on her face and no conditions attached while working many days with debilitating migraines she suffered from all of her life, yet she never complained.

To this day, we thank her for her efforts of changing our lives by guiding us through a complicated and costly immigration process, a process many dream to navigate, even if it's a complex undertaking in our times.

Having experienced the immigration process with Gloria and those Manni helped, I realized that most do not want anything for free. They want to work hard, pay taxes and own a little piece of land to take care of family. They ultimately want to do the right thing, which means paying a reasonable fee to become naturalized in the USA with the pride it deserves.

For this, I thank you, Manni. I hope you're free of migraines in heaven. As for Gloria, your unapologetic secrecy never ceases to amaze me.

15

ZEN LIFE AND HOLLYWEIRD

I cannot imagine the turmoil and struggle Gloria endured as we moved around from one place to another while lacking a plan of any kind. It was clear she was flying by the seat of her pants, on survival mode pulling me along for what looked like an American adventure.

I can't help but wonder, now that I am a mother who treasures the ability of nourishing my thriving teenager by offering her dedicated attention every time she needs it with unconditional love, adoration, structure and routine, what Gloria valued most while raising me, while doing her best to raise her child in two countries and being distracted with her next move, our survival.

Manni's brother, Silvio, the most bitter family member in Gloria's family, arrived in Los Angeles just when I was beginning to find comfort in my pleasant routine with the Hundleys'.

Silvio's arrival and grouchiness entailed Gloria and me vacating the room we shared at the Hundleys,' leaving us to again pack and leave for our next temporary destination, ending my short but colorful time in West Hollywood.

Silvio made no apologies for the inconvenience he caused his cousin, Gloria, when he arrived without notice and consideration. Instead, he exuded a strange sense of cockiness and a very unattractive entitlement stance.

I have always found people to be fascinating and interesting. Even the most boring individual can intrigue me by observing their quirks and patterns, always giving a sense of who they are. However, Silvio's entitled and stubborn ways were uncomfortable to watch considering his extremely humble beginnings. He was unapproachable to me, so I decided to watch his unreasonable character traits while finding the comedy in his acts.

Using comedy and sarcasm helped me make sense of strange and sometimes painful situations such as Silvio, who acted and walked the earth like he was better than the earth itself for no particular reason other than....well, I have yet to know. Unfortunately for Gloria, who also takes herself much too seriously, she never found the humor in Silvio's childishness. Instead, she doubled down taking stances against his actions, only resulting in a deeply hurt and resentful Gloria. To this day, Gloria struggles with this attitude. Their strife is one that belongs in a *novela*.

Years later I read a saying: "Holding a grudge is like drinking poison and waiting for the other person to die," immediately reflecting on Gloria and Silvio. I would venture to guess the genesis of their feud is long forgotten. What is alive and well are their stern and stubborn ways while drinking their poison waiting for the other to drop, all while losing sight of what is really important in life.

So once again, Gloria and I packed and said our "see you laters" to all as we walked to the bus stop on Santa Monica Blvd with our suitcases in each hand hoping the bus was empty enough to ease our belongings through the narrow, busy aisles and occupied seats, finally settling next to a window focusing my eyes on the changing neighborhoods we passed through on the way to Studio City.

The bus trip was short and hot as we melted in sweat arriving in the Valley, soon to be relieved by the water mist that cooled us. The mist playfully nourished the abundantly lush Bali-inspired landscape and secluded villa that would become our next temporary home in Studio City.

Mrs. Sushila would be our next host, a friend of Mrs. Hundley's and owner of the beautiful, serene, meditative oasis I'd be lucky to reside in.

Mrs. Sushila was also from India. She was old and frail, watchful and meditative as she floated through the single-level house from room to room like an angel in what seemed to be a trance. She always wore her salt and pepper hair back in a low ponytail and wore beautiful Indian-patterned silk robes and Kurtis, much like Mrs. Hundley.

The house offered water fountains, dreamcatchers, incense,

praying pillows throughout and a statue I later learned was called Buddha seated by the front door on the ground next to a basket for shoes. The house exuded calm, peace and Zen, bringing anyone's heart rate down, particularly Gloria's.

Experiencing her in this calm state allowed me to discover a side of her I had not seen. It was refreshing and calming to see. I was able to observe the forced permission this healing house gave her without asking. And although we typically didn't speak much, the house offered Gloria and me a time to reflect and just be.

I learned that silence and meditation bring peace and clarity, and clarity offers answers and answers are what I received from this healing home.

It was in Studio City that I began to get clear about the notably peculiar relationship Gloria and I were living. While she bore pain in pushing me out of the canal, fed, clothed, gave me shelter and also worked hard to give me a better life than what she was given, on the downside, and without her knowing, she was never able to nurture and mother me like every child deserves. Perhaps because she had not been nurtured or loved herself; nonetheless, this was the clarity I needed that would help me avoid taking her lack of nurturing personally as I had been.

When clarity is up close and personal, it looks like seeing through a sparkling clean glass window free of all distracting specks. I was able to see how vastly different we both were from each other, bringing a cloud of sadness and solemnness realizing I not only lacked a father figure, but also a mother one. That outside of enjoying delicious enchiladas and rice and beans as our favorite meal, we had minimal in common. Her heart has always been guarded, while mine has always been open to receive. She hugs with closed arms, while I open mine wide and follow with a kiss. She sorrows when I hope;

she is as negative as I am forever and eternally positive. She is short and I'm tall. She is cautious, while I prefer to trust. She is sad when I choose to be happy. She gives with conditions, while I give and forget. She sits, while I need to dance. She keeps secrets, and I am an open book. She lives in the past; I use the past as a learning experience for the future. She's a victim, while I'm victorious. And as sad and lonesome as all this felt, a lightness surged through my being knowing that God put us together for a divine reason that might someday be revealed. For now, I needed to accept her for who she was.

Mrs. Sushila and her calming Zen house would also offer me priceless gifts. The biggest gift was peace found in silence and that in silence I can find answers. Meanwhile, our time in Studio City would come to an end far too soon, and as usual, Gloria would not inform me of our next stop until the day of.

The next move would be the first and only time Gloria and I lived alone in America, and it was the most mind-numbing and bizarre scenarios thus far.

Gloria managed to rent a studio for us in the heart of Hollywood. The studio was one of twenty. Ten studio apartments attached to one another on the North side, the other ten on the South side facing each other divided by a long, barely landscaped center. The units were unadorned and sterile enough to feel like a correctional community.

Living in Hollywood was not the issue. Hollywood is eccentric, wacky and fun offering a melting pot of characters screaming obscenities and laughing at themselves. There's always something or someone interesting to watch. The issue was the layout of the building, the people in it who never spoke to one another that was uneasy and unsafely uncomfortable to which Gloria instructed:

"No hables con nadie cuando llegues de las escuela, y cierra

la puerta."
"Don't speak with anyone after you arrive from school and close the door."

Like that was a reasonable way for a teenage girl to live.

I had been fortunate to experience extraordinarily humble beginnings in Mexico, but I never felt as unsafe as I did while living in what I'm convinced was a provisional interim community, maybe the reason why Gloria could afford the rent. Either way, I pleaded with her to pull another move out of her hat of tricks, and when my plea and wishes were not considered, I retaliated the best way I could.

Up until this time, I was a good kid while reviewing a snapshot of my life with Gloria; this was however my safety, or lack of, so I retaliated not as teen throwing a tantrum, but as a human being wanting to be heard. I stopped coming home when I was supposed to and got lost exploring the neighborhood that felt safer than the correctional facility we lived in. On days she was off from work, I skipped school from time to time while continuing my unspoken protest until she realized I wanted out of that building, NOW.

Gloria may have very well been working on her next move while I was throwing my quiet tantrum, but the fact that she never communicated with me about what was to come next was frustrating, so I did what I had to do.

Ask and you shall receive! Gloria in her quiet, secretive ways rekindled her friendship with Mr. and Mrs. Start in Los Feliz, whom she lived with prior to my existence.

The hills of Los Feliz, a beautiful place to live with stunning Los Angeles's glistening views and great memories to come.

16

LOS FELIZ

It's the little things, the little steps in life that, if we are aware enough, move us forward to a new life and free the soul, particularly in a new country. Even when the journey entails hills, highs and lows, it is the freedom and discovery in the journey we must hang onto and learn from. Otherwise, why do anything?

The 180 and 181 metro bus line became our most permanent form of transportation to our new neighborhood of Los Feliz.

The hills of Los Feliz were inviting and mysterious every time we walked up the two curved hills from our usual bus line drop-off on Los Feliz Blvd.

It wasn't a long walk; it was the hill that kept us fit and huffing and puffing, only to be greeted by the city light views blinking over the porch every night when we arrived home. And on a clear, beautiful day, downtown LA to the Pacific Ocean showed off its best assets, and when clear enough, a little bump of Catalina.

We often carried groceries, water or bags of some sort filling our lives with stuff as the hill kicked our butts every time, but the views were always worth the struggle.

Mr. Start and the missus, who everyone called Mrs. Janice, were our most permanent hosts and also friends of the Hundleys. The connections all began to make sense.

Gloria found part-time work with the Starts and other families throughout Los Angeles, making this our home and a school for me to attend permanently.

Mr. Start was a tall, introverted, handsome pilot. He always kept to himself while giving me the occasional nod of approval every time we crossed paths throughout the house, while Mrs. Janice was an artist, an avid smoker and stricter than most hosts I had come across.

Mrs. Janice's artwork, music and décor had a bit of an Indian flare offering works of inspiration and sometimes touching on world politics.

The best part of the house was the basement that was unlike a basement in the sense of the word. Because the house was on a hill, the basement faced the city side offering lots of light from ceiling to floor glass windows, a perfect room for an artist.

The basement had a darkroom where Mrs. Janice developed raw 35 mm film, a truly unique and treasured task she commanded me to do. The long, tall and wide basement was also filled with paintings, silk art, brushes, photos, fabrics and artifacts of all kinds. Stuff came in and out of there every week.

To this day, I don't know where Gloria found these wonderful artist and cultured friends. All I know is that I LOOOOVED the brain candy. I felt I was making up for lost time.

At the Starts, Gloria and I created consistency and stability, at least I did. Our room was a long, rectangular space next to the basement studio, darkroom and restroom.

Gloria created a small kitchen space with a mini-refrigerator, toaster, an electric two-burner and small shelves for enough plates, glasses and utensils for us to get by. If we craved a more intricate meal, the upstairs kitchen was always up for grabs, a more pleasing option considering the city views. It was a no-brainer; the option to cook in a basement or in a legitimate kitchen with city views is not hard to figure out.

Walking half a mile up and down Los Feliz hills to my most consistent school with my beloved Walkman listening to George Michael, The Cure, Michael Jackson and soundtracks included a happy prance from time to time. I loved the variety that soundtracks had to offer while staying fit and studying old-school Los Feliz homes. Surrendering to a smooth structure in our new neighborhood was welcomed and appreciated.

During my high school years, Mrs. Janice took it upon herself to assign me chores. Chores? I asked as she began to write a list.

What are chores? I wondered.

Why is she making a list? Gloria never made one, I thought.

Who does she think I am, the maid?

There were a lot of reasons why I became angry, confused and rebellious when she decided to implement things into my new routine.

The first would be that I'd never had chores besides cleaning my teeny house in Mexico. Two, Mrs. Janice was not my mother. Three, how did she decide what to put on the list? Four, why did I have to follow her schedule and why couldn't I do them when I wanted to? Five, hormones.

No one had discussed tween and teenage years with me and all that came with it. It never occurred to Gloria to discuss that lovely stage in a girl's life called "a period," much less chores. I was mad.

It wasn't a surprise I resisted "the list." All I wanted to selfishly do was to watch and learn, at least that's what I thought was best because, yes, that's how teenagers think. Teenagers know it all.

After the tantrum passed and I calmed my spoiled, perplexed self, I succumbed to my duties. I had no choice, we lived in her house.

TO-DO LIST:

1. Walk Andrew twice a day.

> Andrew was Mrs. Janice's extremely tall, gray and black greyhound.

> Alongside the dog that bit my finger in Mexico, my dog experience was none, so to be assigned a dog walker for an animal the size of a pony was as bad as a blind date with someone who might as well have spoken Swahili. It took patience, observation, convincing, pulling, cleaning up and waiting for one another until we both found our rhythm. He showed me which side of the street he wanted to launch his

daddy long legs, while I led the way through the hills of Los Feliz.

Soon, Andrew showed his sweet, kind yet stubborn ways, and I learned to let his personality show up as we got to know each other.

2. Water the plants upstairs and downstairs.

In Mexico, every bucket of water was a precious commodity, and it had a specific purpose. Water was not taken for granted, as in many regions of the world.

This task was a tough one to swallow. The concept of watering plants as instructed was often done with sadness and a slight touch of anger.

The entrance, deck and downstairs next to my bedroom were indeed colorful, lush and green. I understood that landscape could bring a calm to the soul. The shapes, colors and types of foliage were abundant, fresh and soothing, but I could not understand why the plants had to be so thirsty every day. I couldn't help but think about families and kids in the world who would have loved to drink accessible water even if it was from a dirty hose.

It was my task. I had no choice, so I made the best of it and often asked Andrew to accompany me along the water-hosing task throughout the house, but of course, he often chose to sit on his ass inside where it was cool.

3. Weekends in Griffith Park.

The animal duty escalated without my knowing. In addition to walking a greyhound the size of a pony and wasting water on plants that needed it again and again, there came a horse.

The day Mrs. Janice informed me I needed to help clean up at Griffith Park, I couldn't help but think it was odd to have to clean a "park" on a weekend. I did go along with no questions asked, and only my imagination wondering what type of park near a nice neighborhood of Los Feliz needed our help. I was more perplexed when we pulled up to dusty, stinky stables filled with beautiful and powerful horses all standing tall and cocky while being walked, groomed, massaged, caressed and loved.

Little did I know Mrs. Janice's concept of "park cleanup" involved picking up heavy pounds of horseshit or scraping it out of their hooves. I was told we were going to "Griffith PARK," not a horse stable.

Mrs. Janice assertively but kindly managed to win the chore list battle with me. I pleaded walking Andrew first thing in the morning might be too much for him, but she put her foot down and said, "No, Karina, he needs to stretch and poop." I suggested I water lightly in the evening and save water; she insisted midday and that was that. I did give up with the horse after I realized I actually enjoyed stable life and the selflessness one has to offer to it and that sometimes being one with a horse is easier than being one with humans. After much cautiousness when walking, brushing and grooming the giant masterpieces, I learned they are not only stunning and strong, but highly intuitive, and if I could learn to read the way they do, I'd be all right.

I did not intend to be a spoiled brat, defiant and stubborn with Mrs. Janice; however, what is a hormonal teen to do when moving around from home to home in a new country, new language and these new things called chores. I realize it could have been worse, and I think she understood my struggle.

Much to my surprise, I never foresaw that walking Andrew, the horse, picking up their shit and watering plants would have their payoffs when Mrs. Janice granted me car access, as long as I ran errands for her during my driving practice.

She reinforced with instruction and practice exactly how my high school driving class covered it, and frankly, God only knows how I would have learned otherwise because to this day, Gloria does not drive.

The bus was great, but the freedom to explore through town

in a car even if Los Angeles traffic can elicit therapy sessions from time to time, was worth the poop, walks and chores.

After a while, these torturous chores ironically became therapeutic. Barn life was messy, dusty and stinky, yet I looked forward to the quietness, the horses and the process they required. Horse life is its own world, and I am blessed to have had the experience of its goodness, even with the manure stink after every visit.

In addition, I accompanied Mrs. Janice into her world of art. Art events and fabric showrooms I helped with were a nice change of pace. My favorite task was the dark, quiet and creative time spent developing the 35 mm film in the dim, scented room of the basement.

Mrs. Janice and Gloria still live together. Their company and friendship have grown with time. Struggles and wrinkles cover their petite, frail bodies, ultimately providing great companionship for one another.

Gloria clearly missed the mothering guidance and the nurturing gene every child deserves; however, she did exemplify an honorable and ethical work ethic to this day, at 79 years old.

As for Mrs. Janice, it would be many moons later and being a mother myself that I'd realize the impact she had in my life without her knowing that led me to never take big or small positive gestures toward others for granted, even strangers.

It is in those unconditional moments when taking selfless time to care for others that we can positively change the world.

LA MIGRA

Los Feliz gave us consistency and structure, what some would call "a routine," an essential ingredient for preserving my sanity.

We moved into a pleasant flow as I began to find my way along my new life, feeling tired, grateful and honored for a place to finally call home.

School work and studies became challenging and daunting in finding a way to make up for lost time, lost lessons and missed school work as a result of moving from town to town, teacher to teacher, school district to another with Gloria. And of course, she had no clue.

I realized the fun adventure of exploring a new country and a new language had its consequences by hurting my academics. I did not have the advantage of being in one particular school, its drama and all that comes with the experience. The dances, sleepovers and the milestones tweens and teens explore were missed along the adventure.

The struggle was intimidating while I adapted to daily homework, reports and tests I had not been subjected to at this level before, which forced me to adapt using my own ingenuity. This became a fire in my belly knowing I had to make it work, but it almost didn't when Gloria dropped the ball and casually told me we may be deported. She forgot to renew our paperwork.

Naturalized Americans who never have to deal with the US

Immigration and Naturalization Service could not fathom what it is like, even with sympathy, and Gloria added to the scenario.

Our pleasant flow was now on eggshells. The savvy and resourceful Gloria comfort zone got the best of her when she realized our expiration date in the US meant we needed to plead to a judge. I didn't know what that all meant; all I knew was I couldn't go back to Mexico. I had gotten a taste of a better life, and I wanted to keep tasting.

I have never prayed harder than during this trial in my life. I prayed that our paperwork would be renewed and my life to continue in America. I prayed until my knees hurt and I ran out of words, which didn't matter because I was certain God knew what was in my heart. He knew my request better than I could ask for it. I prayed promising to never request anything like this again, and of course that was a lie, but I put it in there anyway.

By a miracle of God, lots of money to our immigration attorney and sweet, gentle eyes to the judge, we were granted a renewal, and my stomach could now digest food. I had been a nervous wreck, a walking zombie.

I tried not to be mad at Gloria, but was hard to be ok with her ongoing lack of information. I promised I would always be on top of my paperwork thereafter and would become an American citizen on my own terms as soon as I could.

If I was not in school or checking off my chores or working at the local supermarket after school saving money for my big plan, I was with a guy named Jon.

Jon was a handsome work of art. I met him while bagging his groceries. Jon was tall, utterly beautiful, genuinely nice, easy-going and extremely gentle on the eyes. He was an LA model offering sharp cheekbones, a perfectly crafted jawline and luscious lips. He was *that guy,* and he came to me.

We met one late night when he came across the grocery check-line I was assigned to. He made eye contact, followed by a dashing smile that froze me with shyness. He said a sweet "hello," with a calm, unassuming demeanor enough for me to respond and be smitten with my first official stomach butterflies tickling my core. Jon began to frequent the supermarket, splitting up his shopping needs and requiring more visits to see me while building a rapport. Familiarity began to build during those late nights I was assigned "shopping carts collection" in the parking lot, while he came along for the conversation and company.

We began as casual friends meeting for lunch across the street at the neighborhood Yuka's on Hillhurst, the local taco stand I visit to this day. We typically enjoyed one of their renowned delicious mouth-melting burritos or tacos, and after my shift ended, Jon met me outside the supermarket to walk me home while enjoying a slow pace, talking for hours, finishing off with a make-out session for the night. He had a calm nature that always put me at ease.

Since Gloria worked the same long days, and typically across town, while Mrs. Janice was either writing upstairs or out and about in her art world, Jon begin to join me in the basement to help me with my homework, develop film or simply make out. Life became pretty simple and teenage like.

This went on for some time as we began to mingle in each other's lives with friends and his family, until that one day when our conversation casually moved to drugs, cocaine in particular. Jon openly shared his extremely casual experience with the mysterious white powder.

My mind became foggy with flashbacks of every time we had

been together. I was trying to remember a time when he was off, high or not himself. I was looking for moments he had exhibited traits I had heard about cocaine users. He spoke of it with such an ease and honesty, ultimately offering me some like he was offering Coca-Cola, and interestingly enough, I said, "Sure, why not?"

The next week, he was gone for a modeling gig and returned with a blue vial of white talcum in his hand.

"Here you go, just a little is enough," he said as he placed it on the counter, reaching for a hug after his long departure.

We went upstairs, said hello to Gloria and Mrs. Janice and headed out for the night to see his brother and girlfriend, all while I was completely consumed by the little blue vial left behind on the counter like an aspirin.

Upon our return, I was utterly perplexed that I had this illegal thing in my belongings, but surprisingly, I was uninterested to snort the foreign toxic powder made in God knows where with God knows what chemicals by God knows who. I opened it and felt the white, fine powder while rubbing it between my thumb and middle finger, amazed that this little cobalt blue bottle was indeed illegal, and if I did partake in its side effects, it would be the first illegal act I would consciously say yes to. The very next thought was the distaste for secrecy. I was no fan of that. The hiding behind the selling, purchasing or the snorting it alone or with like-minded company. The entire product, secrecy and act still baffles me, as any illegal drug would baffle me, all of which ultimately hurt lives.

My common sense had a quick conference about that pretty blue vial. I placed the darling cobalt bottle on a counter in Mrs. Janice's darkroom and simply forgot about it because making out with Jon seemed more interesting, more present and fun at the time.

Years later, returning to visit Mrs. Janice and Gloria, I found that infamous vial rolling around the basement. I opened it to again feel the texture and smell it, and I realized I had wasted Jon's time and resources when he offered to get it for me. I always knew I would never do such an illegal act. I think I just wanted to see it.

Being that the bottle had moved from one side of the studio to the darkroom and to the bathroom, my biggest concern and embarrassment became Mrs. Janice. I would die if she thought I had been so stupid to snort anything up my nose besides saltwater. As for Gloria, I'm certain she didn't know what the blue vial was other than it was a pretty cobalt color. I picked it up and threw it in the trash.

My days ended with handsome Jon after he took a lucrative modeling job in New York, with no return or make-out sessions in the near future. We talked on the phone as often as we were able to until the calls shrunk to none.

I missed his company and stories about the crazy modeling world. I left the supermarket for a more lucrative job at the local health food store until I met the next lineup of boys, and that's when it got interesting and just plain stupid.

NUMBNUT #1 - LIAR, LIAR, PANTS ON FIRE

It became necessary to make a strong shift, a required need to change my imprint, the stamp that my childhood story was given. The peace in the conviction to positively nourish my offspring from the womb took its own healing journey. It began without my knowing.

I have always wondered about that time we spent incubated in the womb, when the mother imprints her stamp in our vulnerable state without our choosing. Those forty weeks when we ingest all that she offers. The food and drinks she takes in on our behalf. The sadness, happiness and stress she shares with us as embryos, as we become the form of a human being, all while we soak in all that she is. And then, there's that first day the two meet, when eyes lock, one in dire need of emotional and physical nourishment, while the other, the mother, is presented with a choice of the kind of nurturer she chooses to become.

Gio was 100 percent Latino, a few years older than I, and he would be the one to take my virginity.

Gio and I met through mutual friends of Jon. Gio was a smooth operator. He was a slick, savvy Rico Suave topped with world-class liar and cheater qualities. He was a professional at his craft, like the best man at the poker table, or like it was his job and he got paid well. He orchestrated his shenanigans on the side illustrating the classic "Latin lover" stereotype. I was in for a treat.

Rico Suave was very proud of his car, an odd trait of arrogance for me to accept since material things of the world had shown me there is typically a façade behind the show and that "things" or monetary pride of any manner can separate human beings from one another.

His treasured four wheels managed to transport us around town in lover's lane for most of our three years, along with the other ladies he had on the side when I was working or in school.

On the upside, because there is always an upside as far as I'm concerned, his family became mine, particularly during those fun Latino and American traditions Gloria and I rarely shared.

Gio was the oldest of three boys. His family lived in a busier side of Hollywood filled with gates, traffic, freeways and roughness of a certain kind. It was not like my humble neighborhoods in Mexico, or the suburbs of Houston or even Los Feliz. It was a neighborhood with its own pulse offering enough eye candy and learning experiences to keep me safe and take me into the future. A much-needed taste of "street smart."

His mother, Rita, was a horse of a different color. She was blunt, tough, sharp and brutally honest with an overshadowed side of gentle and good shown only in quiet, alone moments. Her voice was raspy and loud enough to set me straight from the beginning. She offered daily doses of abrasive and humorous common sense ending with personal digs, always finishing with *pinche* or *cabrona,* funny or offensive words, depending on the relationship and mood in how they are used. Not the kindest compliments if one takes herself too seriously, yet eye opening if one pays attention.

Rita's left-handed, sarcastic compliments were quick enough to miss, but I was often reminded of the point she made by her mischievous laughter. She had no shame. She ran the show.

All in all, her bottom line had a sweet, frosty layer of care and love leaving most to realize "the act" was her translation and expression of love and affection. After much observation, a lot of listening and being the recipient of her type of communication, I realized she was Gloria of another kind, with a different force of nature and tenacity. Rita offered me the "aha" moment, an epiphany that would be priceless and a lifelong lesson about how human beings show their own versions of love. A lesson I could not have learned in school, and one that serves me to this day.

I am a firm believer that we, humans, are born with love in us; there is no question about it. It begins in the womb. Most often, love is taught by the parents we're given, or not. Either way, we are all born with it and provided many choices and opportunities to see, experience and exhibit our own versions of love. It is always up to us to hide it or let it radiate. This was Rita's way.

During my time with Gio, and while working at the health food store, his cousin, Alma, set off to Yale to begin a higher level of education. Yale seemed so far to me, prestigious and intangible at the time. While excited for her journey to see and experience another part of America on her own, it became an opportunity to execute my exit plan.

High school came and went, like a required task never to be thought of after. It was a must for Gloria, while never touching on anything higher thereafter, as if high school was reaching high, and her job was done, but not until she took the picture to prove it. The Greek Theater was a beautiful venue for the money shot, cap, gown and diploma in hand to snap for proof.

By then, funds from my days at the supermarket, endless babysitting and running errands for others accumulated enough to finally set me off on my own, to unfold my own journey as a lost child of God and a vagabond in the City of Angels. I was ready.

When one is hungry and ready, one gets creative, and it didn't take me much effort to approach Gio's auntie, offering her a little rent money for Alma's room while helping around the house until I found a full-time job.

I remember a slight apprehension that made me nervous enough to press her with a conviction I've grown to nurture. It's the same conviction when it feels like my gut is right; it's the right move.

I didn't give her a choice to respond as she agreed with hesitation while considering both of our struggles. That I was leaving my mother, and her child was leaving her.

My yearning to be on my own was my greatest desire. I didn't mind nor did I consider the essential factor, that my survival would be based on minimum wage, or that I lacked a car for transportation. It did not matter one bit, nothing matters when one's will is strong enough to get things done. I knew there were jobs to be had, and there were many buses for me to hop on.

I find "teenage" time riveting, complex and utterly fascinating, a time when we know it all. This stage often possesses a slightly scared tickle in the belly, with an uncanny drive unlike any other. A drive and desire to be free because, after all, we know it all. This is a time when safety and one's livelihood are not questioned. Nothing is questioned. You just do it because that's how the teenaged mind works, and that was my only option at the time. *I am invincible, and I can do it on my own.*

A few weekends after high school graduation, I walked out with all I needed, all of the most essential belongings stuffed in my high school backpack, including my *Thomas Guide*.

I left Gloria with great peace. It was not the stereotypical teenage rebellion, or a tantrum or anger for that matter because I didn't know what anger was YET. My leaving was about a conviction that Gloria had done what she could and I was letting her off the hook. Our bond was broken by my will to rise to the next level and the level after that, and she couldn't take me there. But she brought me here, to America, and for that, I am forever grateful.

I left Los Feliz with that teenage hunger we never get to experience again. I was alive and kicking, excited for whatever was to come knowing with great confidence that God would be next to me. So I left and immediately searched for jobs like it was my livelihood, because it was. I needed to work to feed myself, and when there is a will strong enough, there is always a way. For me, it was God's way, so He took me to my next job, the local health food store, where I would learn a newfound love for wellness, vitamins and health.

While working and expanding my new wellness addiction, I began to notice Gio was spending too much time in the mall, and not necessarily for work or shopping purposes.

There is gullible, and there is just plain stupid, and stupid I was not when I began to nurture that lovely intuition every female is born with. I didn't know what it was; maybe it was the vitamins I was taking because I could not put the feeling in words. It was like a cloud following me with no break, an itch that needed relief leading me to investigate and follow his trail until the one day I nailed him.

After following his careless routine and steps along the wide hallways of the mall, I had the pleasure of meeting one of the girls with whom Gio was cheating. It was that easy, and he that stupid.

Thank God for God's grace that came over me when I approached the young girl, while taking great observation of her character and interaction with her customers. I wanted to see who she was and gauge her smarts before I confronted her with my newfound anger, yet it was compassion that ran through my bones. Ironically and sadly enough, the poor girl had no idea Gio was cheating on her, and interestingly enough, I felt for her. We were both being played by a true cheating operator who lost his game by a girl with no car.

At this time, we were engaged. We had no business being engaged, but I said yes because it wasn't an "I do." His newfound extra-curricular activities made me wonder how long I'd tolerate this type of dysfunction, the cheating game. If this happens while engaged, what happens later, I wondered?

After confronting Gio with clear timelines, events and perfected P.I.-quality facts, it was all not good enough to accept. Gio mustered up *cojones* large enough to reject my findings with liar's conviction only talent of his kind could practice.

So I continued to visit her storefront wondering if they were going along with their indiscretion, only to realize I was now the numbnut for forgiving him and playing his game. I was colluding in his betrayal while walking around with grief and insecurity like his puppet.

It was then when I wondered just so ever so lightly where that came from. Where does cheating come from? Where's the genesis? And for Gio, why?

I refused to file it under "we were young" because, even though we were, it was too easy an excuse.

I couldn't help to wonder if *cheating* was a gene, or was it an imprint from the womb or from a parenting lack? How does one learn or want to cheat? Is it learned behavior?

The task and heartache were much too hurtful and heavy to dissect during what were supposed to be fun, youthful years, so I ended the relationship, the one that unfortunately took my virginity after three years. I did gain great family memories and a lifelong friendship with his brothers, Mike and Luke. And thanks to social media, we now connect and cheer our growth by a simple "like" or encouraging comments.

Breaking up is never fun. Breaking up forces one to shift, change and grow *if* we're awake enough, which I was not. I was asleep in my existence, moving through life trying to survive while securing a roof over my head and food for my tummy, a task that brought me more pleasure than chasing after an infant who was chasing a cat's tail.

I ended my time with Gio's auntie to fully detach from his world, and I moved along to motels, hotels and spare rooms before Airbnb was a thing. But it wouldn't take long until another knucklehead knocked on my door because I was on a roll, after all. I was sleepwalking and leaving myself open to the next numbnut, so here I go again.

NUMBNUT # 2 - ALCOHOL AND WELLNESS ARE AN OXYMORON

There is no such thing as a coincidence. Some call it luck, opportunity, circumstance, chance or karma. The list of names people use is endless. I call it "God's way of communicating with us." Albert Einstein wrote, "Coincidence is God's way of remaining anonymous." Bottom line, pay attention when coincidence crosses your path because everything happens for a reason.

After a lengthy time working at the local health food store, I learned about wellness and the importance of local produce. I learned about vitamins, herbs, safe ingredients, wheatgrass and bee pollen I ingested like it was my business, in the 1990s, before these trendy times. I also learned that I liked it ALL. The fact that a vitamin, turmeric or a specific ingredient has a very particular effect was fascinating enough to change what I knew about food and traditional medicine. My newfound interest took my attention for reading every vitamin, food, herb and health bible we sold during slow, late nights. But it was Christine Northrup's original *Women's Bodies, Women's Wisdom* that impacted my outlook for the rest of my life, and one that will hopefully buy me a few more years of health.

Those days of chasing Gio's indiscretions through the mall became essential in combining two new interests in my life.

Following his trail through cosmetic departments that exuded pretty scents, displays of makeup, lotions and potions became a heaven I wanted get lost in, and one I could combine with my new wellness love. So I applied to the nicest department store in the mall and dressed in my most professional outfit my vagabond days allowed, with a little blush, mascara and lipstick to fit the bill.

This is where I met Mitra, my new Estee Lauder counter manager. She was the cutest thing on earth. Tiny, gentle, girly and really easy to be with. Mitra had a small room for rent, to which I quickly said, "I will be your roommate" without her asking. I needed a closer and permanent place to live, while knowing full well it was God who had delivered the very fitting opportunities.

Mitra was a great roommate and person to be around. We were both low-key and quiet in our lifestyle, and from time to time, dancing was on our minds. For a strange reason, this one time, we headed inland.

Angelenos typically head west for many reasons, if not all. To enjoy and live closer to the beach, or to the west side where trendy bars reinvent themselves, and socializing is chic while enjoying the happenings of Los Angeles. Why we headed inland to dance I'll never understand. It was the first and the last time I headed east for dancing in particular. The only other reason I would now head inland would be to drive through to Palm Springs or for a great new taco or tamale restaurant in East LA, downtown or Boyle Heights; otherwise, it is not common to go inland for any reason.

So Mitra and I headed to a happening, kicking club by the 10 Fwy. "Kicking" because it was a kicking fest of people stomping their heels, with hands on their waists dancing a perfectly orchestrated lineup to Billy Ray Cyrus's "Achy Breaky Heart." As we walked in, the ground vibrated each time they kicked and turned in sync mesmerizing me enough to forget I had entered a cowboy bar, inland, just off the 10 Fwy. To top it off, Mitra and I were the only Latinas in sight. The entire moment was foreign.

After much observation and realization there would be no dancing for me because I had never heard of line dancing before, and while digesting this new breed of people I had never encountered, "country music people," one of them tapped me on the shoulder asking me to dance. This is when I met Kyle, my next pathetic boyfriend and country music lover to boot.

Kyle was your typical Caucasian charming cowboy fella, with a perfect charm to distract the gullible, and because I had not learned enough from Gio, I fell for it.

We chatted and flirted until Mitra and I were tired, realizing we had to work the next morning, and now we had to drive a long way home, westbound.

Our drive back was laughs and giggles about the random club we had encountered filled with cowboys, line dancing and achy breaky hearts.

Next morning, while slightly tired and piling makeup on to hide the fact, the phone rang across the makeup counter from mine with a Kyle on the line. Mitra gave me her sweetest glance and flirty eyes and said: "OMG, he likes you. He tracked you down so fast. You met twelve hours ago." I reached for the phone, a bit smitten and disturbed by his aggressiveness. This was before Google, cell phones and the various tracking conveniences of our times. I wondered why the rush. It seemed too quick to be flattery, a gut feeling I failed to heed, and one that would bite me in the ass soon enough.

We went on a date the next day, and we immediately became

a thing. He was charming, loving, playful, easy going. After spending many nights over, and with Mitra's permission, he moved in and it all began.

Three's company was fun for a while, but it got a little old, privacy considering, so Kyle and I got our own place not too far away, close enough to Mitra, and far enough that I could walk to work while he worked from our new apartment.

Walking was a great time to meditate to and from work. A time I took for conversations with God and to pump myself up, all while carrying my good friend, "the Walkman," and listening to some of the same, the Boss, The Police, Genesis, George Michael and soundtracks of the movies of those times.

Kyle and I had a simple beginning. We cohabitated and did well for quite some time. Gloria banked on his charm, giving us her Pope blessing after he proposed. We ventured out on short weekend trips, spent time with his circle of social friends that had little to be desired and traveled to Alabama to visit his parents in the new home they had just purchased.

We visited his parents in a rural part of Alabama along the longest road I can remember. From the highest peak, the long two-way road danced to high and low hills dressed with a lushness of trees along each side. Houses sat deep off the road, far away from each other enough to miss screams, murders or celebrations of any kind. The road was smooth, lonesome and rarely traveled. It was perfect for long walks and jogs, and that's what I did while making the best of the boring trip and company his parents offered. I explored this part of America with great curiosity, only to learn that this part of America was not ready for me and would be equally curious about me.

After the third day of quiet jogs and walks along the long road with my faithful Walkman I danced to along the road, through miles and miles of trees and houses, I waved and smiled to anyone who was in their front yard, soon realizing the audience grew every day.

The locals didn't wave or smile when I jogged or walked through their road. Instead, they stared and stood still closer to the road as I passed, with deep frowns leaving me wondering, "Why the face?" I didn't know why the perplexed faces until the end of my boring but very athletic trip, when I realized I never saw a single human being jog in any part of Alabama I visited or speed walk for that matter.

I began to put two and two together, noticing I had been the only running and walking enthusiast they had seen in a while, and probably the only Mexican they'd seen for some time. I was in the Deep South, after all, where ordering a salad was frowned upon unless it was accompanied by buttery grits and biscuits.

When Kyle and I returned to our home life, I soon realized he was an utter dud with charm and had an escalating alcohol habit that showed me the face of a raging alcoholic. I was living with a Jekyll and Hyde of personalities and temper after a thoroughly chewed tin of Copenhagen because alcohol was not enough.

After three years of brainless mind exchange and various cheating indiscretions I discovered at the local cowboy club, it was clear I needed to do something, pronto.

Unfortunately, life had made me accumulate things more than my high school backpack could endure. I now had two boxes of essential items I had grown accustomed to and a rack of clothes I could carry on one arm.

I quickly arranged a temporary stay with a friend in lovely San Marino, Pasadena. I waited for a Tuesday, his traditional cowboy bar night. I planned my perfect exit plan with Mary, my girlfriend, only to be stalled by his returning earlier than usual from the bar, delaying my forever departure until he drank enough beer and spit enough chew until he passed out on the couch. He was that pathetic, and it was that easy. There was no reason to tiptoe around him; he was perfectly drunk for Mary and me to grab my backpack, my two boxes from under the bed and my rack of clothes. I never saw him again; it was a good night.

There was a clear conviction in my soul that I had not come to America to put up with nonsense, particularly a lush with a disgusting chew habit. I had managed to date a compulsive liar and cheater, and now I had added addiction to the list. I was on a roll while learning an immense number of lessons.

I learned about true dysfunction, addiction and what lost souls will do to satisfy their vices. I learned about tactics, manipulation, individual habits, emotional mind fuck and patterns that cheaters, liars and addicts must orchestrate to get what they need. It's a lot of work, but they do it well. Leaving an alcoholic was the easiest and smoothest decision I ever made, and I'm grateful it was that easy.

My days of borrowing and paying rooms by the week at friends' houses or random rooms that came along resumed a new norm, all while Gloria went about her life having no idea what I was up to because she never truly asked.

My hard work and dedication rewarded me from a salesperson to a counter manager. Selling, managing and being surrounded by a billion-dollar beauty industry was an exciting, fresh start, all while catering and working in the Lion's Den filled with women of all ages and types. This is when I learned about the complicated and powerful female of the species. Good times ahead.

DRUGS ARE BORING. LOTIONS & POTIONS ARE FUN!

Working with and for women can bring interesting times, particularly during the time I was ripe, trying to figure out who I was with zero guidance, but with a light from God that always endured and a fire up my ass that kept me hopeful, curious and able.

Confucius said: "Choose a job you love, and you will never have to work a day in your life." I didn't know this then, but I could identify with the sentiment when working with makeup, lotions and potions. It felt like playtime anytime I touched, smelled and shared any product with anyone who listened and allowed me to touch her skin or while dabbing a beautiful blush along forgotten cheekbones. Escaping into the world of colors, smells, textures and ingredients was and is still heaven, especially when sharing this newfound love and knowledge with women in search of a little something to make them feel younger and prettier, the reason why the beauty industry collects not millions, but billions, of dollars.

The beauty industry touches on many senses, results and bottom lines; however, I found the most profound element the industry misses is the vulnerable connection women share when exchanging tips and tricks to beautify one another. It is those moments to be cherished and nurtured while elevating each other. Moments I was blessed to experience and learn about us, the complicated female of the species. The desire to feel good about ourselves can sometimes be solved with a little lipstick, blush or the newest face cream to erase hurt or laughter streaming through valleys of wrinkles, while accentuating beautiful features every woman possesses. These moments are missed in the preoccupation for design, the perfect font and product name. At the end of the day, we're all questing for connection, a shared moment, a touch and validation to raise each other up, observations from a young Mexican girl raising herself.

For me, this would be the time I'd learn about beauty from the outside, later realizing the ultimate goal was to feel good inside. This came to me many years later. In the meantime, I learned about women, their quirks and hang ups exhibited when asking for the perfect serum to lift their beauty spirit. A potion for the unwanted pimple or hydration and glow for the sluggish days we all share, and sometimes it was pure vanity. Ultimately, I learned that women want to be loved, and we're asking in all sorts of ways, even when not feeling worthy.

After long days of working in a mall setting, indoors not knowing whether it was daylight, raining or cold, two girlfriends and I looked forward to the last minute at the end of our shift, that last minute to clock out for the day ready for the night happenings. We had parties and clubs on our minds, never knowing what the night had to offer.

We would head to one of our houses to get dolled up to the nines. We caressed the newest makeup with the smoothest brushes, slather lotions and potions we discovered at work and hit the town with our prettiest hair and sexiest gear.

Nights offered the trendiest clubs, boat gatherings, lingerie parties, swanky bars, chic restaurants, classy cigar rooms and the hottest parties in glass houses and extravagant living grounds I never knew existed. The venues were abundant and endless. Kel and Lara knew the town, the movers and shakers. Access to clubs and tables with bottle service were the norm, and parties offered ocean breezes or dreamy, glistening LA city light views. This was every night, and I thought it was normal.

We typically arrived at whatever venue Kel and Lara had up their sleeve, arriving around eleven or midnight. Being a newbie to the party world, I always worried the party would be over by then because of the late hour. In true fashion, parties of this kind were alive and well, filled with mingling and tingling well past crescent and full moons, and in reality, things were just getting started. Guests were happy, bright, light and high. It was always a spectacle. We were always given a table and let in right away. We never waited in line; I never knew what waiting in line meant until many moons later.

Outings of this kind opened a different Los Angeles. I was able to explore the fun life in the LA party scene and survive without drugs and favors for money. This is when Bar One was happening. The Rainbow Room and The Viper Room were newer and still cool, back when home parties were open all night and layered with white powder, sex and orgies. It was a great time for people watching, and I was a fly on the wall taking it all in almost nightly. The things and acts people partake in when they are high and deep in their drug escape take me aback. I imagine it hasn't changed, and I imagine this was my version of what many reference as "Studio 54" times, but not really since there was no Andy Warhol.

Thankfully for me, besides a cocktail or two, and maybe a shot of tequila, coke or any illegal drugs offered to me did not interest me then, or now. To this day, while still open mind-ed and more grown up, I do not understand sniffing a foreign white powder up my nose, needling my arm or burning a spoon with a strange substance, all of which one has to purchase and use in hiding.

I was coming to terms with pending issues without yet knowing the genesis. I knew something needed fixing and healing, but I had a distinct conviction that a drug was not the solution, that it was wrong in all levels, that it would set me back.

Partying continued for some time, resulting in a bloated body and pimpled pizza-like skin after nights of drinking and eating 3 am meals with enough time to sleep it off, work and do it again. But when the girls and I were there in the moment, happy, dancing and escaping the troubles of life that are now trivial, I enjoyed it immensely. I got lost in the moment dancing all night, alone, in my own mental space of music and dance story turning a crazy night into a therapeutic and mental relief, grasping every moment and never worrying who was looking. I did have to push off the grinders and perverts who interpreted my dancing alone as a girl up for grabs; that was utterly annoying. They were interrupting my fun dance therapy, forcing me to read their intentions while dancing away from their rising penis.

I will give it to those who'd pushed their intentions into my ears: "Do you want a line and f!@&?" To which I'd say: "No, thank you" as I danced away to the other end of the floor.

One has to take forwardness for what it is. It's straight up honesty; it was refreshing, and there is no waste of time. Nothing is better than that. They had an offer, and I was not interested. Was it sexual harassment? YES, but they were thinking with their penis. They were honest about their intentions, and I said no. Although I had been abandoned, sexually abused and now with two failed numbnut relationships, feeling verbally assaulted by brutally honest, drug-infused jerks was not going to shake me enough to cry, so I kept dancing.

The girls were always moving around the club. I never knew

what they were up to, but we never left each other. When I got tired and they were not, I looked around for the perfect resting spot.

Resting time was typically the floor in the movie room inside the large party house, the little corner in the boat or a booth at a club. I always found a place to rest while keeping an eye open for the girls or for perverts who may have thought my resting time was their playtime. Until that one day, of course.

I was dating the owner of the club we frequented, who also periodically threw large lingerie parties. Yes, he was that guy, and I was that knucklehead.

One fun evening, while dancing and minding my own fun business, high on music and life, something foreign managed to slip into my drink. I felt it immediately. My existence felt light, dizzy with round and round spins, feeling warm, loose and out of control. I could not hold my body within minutes. My arms were butter while dragging myself outside the club in need for coolness when the owner, the guy I was dating, happened to see my struggle. He saw the vagueness in my eyes and grabbed my friends and me into his beautiful convertible Rolls Royce, driving off on the 405 over the Sepulveda Pass. I remember this because the breeze and open air calmed the spins, cooling me enough to alertness. I stood up as he drove fast through the pass and felt the air sober the intrusiveness of whatever was poured in my drink and my bloodstream. It was an unwelcoming feeling, and I fought hard against it because I knew if I caved and did not forcefully stay alert, something would happen to me.

We arrived at his house, filled with girls in lingerie. The beautiful house jerked me immediately with loud music, alcohol available throughout and too many people to deal with as my head began to feel normal.

I never learned who and what substance was slipped into my delicious drink, and besides my head pounding and waking up to several gals next to me, I seemed to have survived the night, the last night of much mischief, shenanigans and long nights of this kind.

Late next morning after my guy left for work, I tried to make sense of the kitchen and happenings from the night before. I knew I'd had enough. I called Gio's brother to pick me up and said goodbye to late nights, 3 am eating and LA nights I escaped with dancing memories and funny characters along the way.

I was exhausted, but it was all fun.

NUMBNUT #3 - ACTOR AND GOD INVASION

Why do we do the things we do? I've always wondered, particularly when we get the same nonproductive or useless results. My head doctor says the genesis goes back to the womb, my mother, and I don't disagree entirely, but I don't want to make her an excuse for repetitive poor decision making on my end. It's too convenient and lazy. There has to be accountability for growth; it can't always be someone else's fault.

Albert Einstein wrote, "Insanity is doing the same thing over and over again and expecting different results." He also said, "We cannot solve our problems with the same thinking we used when we created them." I say that sometimes we don't know there's a problem big enough to have to change until we hit bottom. And sometimes, we're simply lazy in the head because change is hard.

And that is why I stumbled upon the third pathetic relationship because I hadn't yet realized I had issues big enough to have to solve them. It would take two more years of my life before I began to get real with it all, before I hit bottom.

On a slow, quiet morning, Michael stumbled across my beauty counter eliciting attention that required little effort. Michael was a different one. He was quick witted, funny, unnecessarily loud, lacking a bit of couth, but he was charming. He lit up a room with his dashing smile, striking features touched by his surfer dirty blond hair and dreamy blue eyes, ingredients for an actor, which he was.

He persisted for weeks until I caved. It was hard to beat the personality and looks, forgetting to look at the inside, again.

After borrowing bedrooms from friends and acquaintances for a few months, and after having left numbnut #2 and now a new guy on the books, it was time to find a permanent place of my own.

I discovered Burbank during my search for hikes, when I found Wildwood Canyon Park. Beautiful and complex hikes hid behind The Castaway Restaurant and DeBell Golf Course. I hiked every little trail I could, sometimes getting lost but always finding my way to the tip, surrendering to nature, beautiful sunsets and city light views. I loved those hikes and the healing they offered me. Those views took away all my questions and allowed me to escape into silence. Far too soon, I realized I needed to haul ass down the hill before it was too dark to find my way down. It was that mesmerizing.

After one of these dreamy hikes, I headed down the hill to the nearest liquor store in search of the local Burbank paper hoping to find a room for rent inked in the classifieds, while feeling confident that God had a plan, and He did.

I called the first "room for rent" ad. It offered me a room in a clean house on the flat section of Burbank, by the studios, and street parking with modest rent. It seemed like a perfect location with easy access to the 134, the 5 and 101 Fwy next door to my love, Toluca Lake, and let's not forget the Barham Pass that takes you over the hill to the Hollywood Bowl and dumps you on Hollywood Blvd. It was a perfect middle location.

I dreaded holding the public phones in my hand and against my ear, while touching the numbers, but fortunately it took only one call to make the appointment to view the room that held high hopes for me.

The street was lined with beautiful trees touching each other. The home looked cozy from the outside as I rang the bell, nervous that I would not be able to live there, that something may be wrong, but was startled by the force of nature who opened the door.

"Hiiiiiiiiii!!!!!" she said with the enthusiasm of a child having found candy. She was mildly wild; she seemed desperate and scared, a concern quickly overshadowed by her insanely beautiful face. She was gorgeous and still is. I could not keep track of my thoughts or my body as she pulled me into the most nurturing hug anyone had ever given me. She owned her space, and I took it all in with open arms while moving my face away from her crazy curly hair. I melted in her hug but wondered if she was crazy, or if she had the hots for me. I didn't care; I let go and breathed in her loving gesture as long as it lasted.

When we finally let go, and still holding each other's arms, she looked deep into my eyes with great intention, as if she was trying to read me. It felt intrusive but safe. The scene was theatrical but filled with a rare familiarity and rawness. The kind of rawness that is honest and present, the kind that is refreshing or intrusive depending on the recipient. Her name was Pilar, and she was a starving actor.

After gathering ourselves, sharing names and positions, Cathy, the owner, made her way to the front door. She was strange from the get-go, but nothing could compare to Pilar's introduction. Cathy was Pilar's polar opposite. There was no hug, only a jelly-like handshake, one that barely touches fingers, making me wonder why she even bothered. She quickly showed me the house, the main areas I would be allowed to use, the kitchen, the bathroom and laundry. But it was the kitchen that should have alerted me to what was to come.

Every kitchen drawer and counter were labeled with names indicating every item that belonged there, and I mean, every item because forks, spoons and knives are not obvious enough; they each had a label. Each size was labeled in the Tupperware cabinet and could only be stacked in twos. The plates had labels, even the obvious stacked bowls. If she could have labeled where feces went, she would have, I'm convinced.

While ignoring the signs compensating with location, a clean house and Pilar, my new forever loving and fascinating friend, I soon realized I couldn't stay there long. Cathy began to walk through the house with plastic bags wrapped around her legs with the intention of sweating and losing weight. Why else would anyone walk around their life with heavy trash bags as pants?

I tried, but the Tupperware and utensil drawer could have sent anyone to therapy, and I already had enough material of my own. I was certainly not going to have a middle-aged plastic bag designer stall my journey, but I stuck it out for a few months. I loved the neighborhood and Pilar.

She and I became inseparable and dear friends immediately. She may not have enjoyed the struggle, but I learned an immense amount of human psychology while accompanying her through endless auditions, and Michael's, who was also a starving actor.

While actors began to stick to me, like bees on honey, I saw how interesting and complex they are, with a fascinating dysfunction that made sense to me, while realizing they were also questing for love, connection, and starving in the process.

After a few months, the plastic-dressed lady of the house drove me out the door. I could not fathom living under her roof any longer. Pilar and I continued to see each other every day and became tighter than ever. Soon after, we found a townhouse off Glenoaks, closer to my hiking trails and lived together for a while.

Pilar was one of the most loving, honest, intentional and raw individuals I had met until then. We got lost in makeup, lotion and potion conversations. We smelled, touched and shared new beauty finds and tips. And still do. We loved food. She loved waking up to my Mexican breakfast and freshly made salsa when she strolled out of her bedroom with her crazy Cuban hair, and I loved when she cooked her *pollo de fricasse,* my favorite Cuban dish.

"Good morning, SUNSHIIIIIIIIIIIINE!!!" I said with a louder than normal squeaky voice every morning.

"You're too loud. I haven't had my coffee," she responded with her silk eye mask covering most of her eyes and most dramatic response.

I was intrigued by the devoted time she spent reading her bible, and I was perplexed when seeing her write in it, making notes and bookmarks throughout. Growing up Catholic, reading the bible or writing in it was almost sacrilegious. They weren't practices I remember growing up and during the time with my angel nun and school priest.

Pilar let me borrow her second bible. "Who has two bibles?" I wondered, but she did, and she invited me to attend her church.

Something happened that Sunday morning. I'd like to say God happened, and it was God, He always happens, but there was more. We walked into the darling church. She greeted parishioners, and I observed the simplicity of God's home and His followers hugging, talking and genuinely engaging one another, most carrying their own bible under their arm. I began to feel light and vulnerable, so I reached for the first seat and kneeled, overtaken by tears and sorrow streaming down my face. I cried for minutes without stopping, and when I finally let go I was lifted, relieved. It can't be explained. I had not gone to church in so long, lost in my ways and now found in one of God's many homes. Emmanuel Church, Pilar and our bible study brought me closer to God than I had even been. I needed it. I needed Him and always will, and meeting Pilar was no coincidence. This was one fine day.

Sometime later, Pilar was excited to invite me to her movie premiere. My blasé response to her invitation slightly angered her, wondering why I was not joyous for her, her movie and the invite. She was taken by my lack of enthusiasm, when in reality I was perplexed.

"Do you mean to say, you are a real actress, like this is a real thing for you?"

"What do you mean?" she asked. And if you knew Pilar, you'd know her tone and understand her baffled response while exhibiting disbelief shown through her beautiful eyes, wondering why I had doubted her.

The exchange did not go well, and calming the misunderstanding was not easy. I shared my newfound experience with inspiring actors, Michael and industry people I had met in parties and clubs, though I had never seen their work. She watched me carefully, smiled and gave me a hug.

That's Pilar. When she senses honesty, she gives you love, but when she smells BS, it's not good.

Mi Familia, her movie, was as real as her profession. It was the first time I'd seen her in her element enjoying her craft and the fruit of her labor.

She auditioned endlessly, and I moved away from cosmetics on to waiting tables at the local, but very popular, coffee shop in Glendale.

Cosmetics was great fun and still is, but after having to turn down a large promotion that required a car I didn't have yet, or moving deeper in the San Fernando Valley, I decided to get outside those walls for something new. I had spent four years inside closed walls, not knowing if it was day, night or raining, which affected me greatly. I began to feel somber and sad. That is the trick with department stores, the lack of windows leading to the outside, the air conditioning and inside visuals set to keep the customer laser focused inside, buying, and us, selling. So I walked across the street to the popular coffee shop, Foxy's, to visit my waitress friend and asked for a job.

Meeting with the owner, Shan, was strange and awkward. He was intimidating and a man of few words, but when he spoke, there was a purpose.

"Why should I hire you? You've never waited tables," he asked with a smirk.

"Because I want to learn here!" I responded while Gato and Freddie, the bus boys, who were brothers, stared holding their coffee pots and water jugs ready to make their refill rounds.

Shan hired me a few days later and taught me everything there was to know about waiting tables, with his usual shortage of words.

"Stay sharp, think ahead and be clean," he said as he handed me Foxy's long menu I had to memorize.

I watched him carefully, particularly when he interacted with guests. He was always at the front of the house. Shan greeted each guest with genuine acknowledgement as he reassured them they were getting the best seat in the house. To him, every seat in the restaurant was the best seat in the house.

Guest birthdays were celebrated tenor style. He belted his best 'happy birthday,' and without being asked, guests refrained from eating as Shan vibrated his best falsetto finishing off to a restaurant filled with applause. Every day there was a birthday, and every day I was blessed to experience the repetitive but blissful rhythm watching the smiles and joy he brought to his guests. But it was his humble grin I rejoiced in as he walked away taking in the applause.

Foxy's was where I came out of my shell and was forced to become personable, while developing sassiness and alertness when dealing with men. Dealing with spoiled, rude and unreasonable guests was difficult to ignore and tough to take. I could have slapped pancakes and steaks across many guests' heads anytime a complaint was not warranted. I wondered if the unreasonable complaint was from their lack of attention as a child because the meal looked perfectly good and I knew I could walk two blocks either way and find a homeless soul happy to have it. Or was the complaint because they were served with silver spoons and Foxy's was a coffee shop? A girl from a little town in Mexico who was raised with very little can simplify the littlest of complaints, a practical and appreciative way to live, but a dangerous one if she wants to have and keep friends.

The restaurant business taught me that people like to complain, and even when the meal is replaced and fixed to perfection, failing the first time will always be remembered.

"Relax, it's part of the restaurant business," Shan would say when I complained about a guest.

"I will never accept that. I don't deserve their spoiled attitude. They're lucky to eat at a restaurant, be served and complain," I'd respond and walk away, pouting.

Thankfully, the positive outweighed these silly, bratty guests who acted like royalty with ill-mannered attitudes toward the help, me and the bus boys, yet somehow, I twisted the story realizing how ridiculous they were. It was not about me; it was them. They must have forgotten where they were because it certainly wasn't Spago or Mastro's. It's a coffee shop, people.

The best were my regulars, guests who waited to sit on the side of the restaurant I was assigned. Regulars became family over those years. Regulars consisted of people like the couple who were on their first date, who got married and had kids. Seeing these life stages was a neat experience for me and hope for my love future. Or the veteran who sat alone and demanded the same seat at the counter every day at 5 pm. He always gave everyone, particularly me, a hard time if the butter was not cold. If his seat counter was taken, he stood behind it until that guest was finished. He stood behind the bar seat close enough for the current guest to fill the energy. He was a true curmudgeon.

There were also the single guys who came in every Sunday morning hungover, looking forward to a sloppy breakfast for recovery.

The old Italian couple who came in every Friday for date night were a joy. The husband wheeled his bride's wheelchair into the restaurant as the bus boys (Gato, Freddie, Cesar, Effi, Juan and the rest) helped to carry her to their favorite booth. They were old, and she was his bride because he treated her like one, with adoring love even in their old age.

Then there was the single guy who ordered the same meal on Tuesdays and Thursdays, and when I approached the counter with his spaghetti and meatballs, I smiled and called his name, "Rich, here's your delicious meal, yuuuummmmm!!!" He loved the attention, and the bus boys thought I was nuts walking away laughing, "pinche Karina."

The Mafioso lookalikes were out of the movies. They drove in large, black Mercedes and sat in the patio dressed in dark suits and ordered pots of coffee, even when it was hot outside. This was Glendale; it was always hot, but they were always respectful, generous and loyal.

I learned this one afternoon when a younger group of males spoke and gestured inappropriately to me.

"Is this their usual behavior?" the main Mafioso lookalike asked.

"Typically, they're not very nice," I said, pouring his coffee.

The younger group finished their meal, paid and walked to the parking lot not knowing the Mafioso lookalikes were following.

"Do you know them?" I asked, when the Mafiosos returned to their table.

"They'll never bother you again," the main Mafioso responded while resuming his coffee.

"Oh, thank you," I answered, slightly concerned, smitten and protected for once.

The younger group never bothered me again because I never saw them again, and that was that.

After a couple of years, I pleaded to be the night manager when the opportunity presented itself. Shan discouraged me suggesting I would hate missing out on my nightlife. Being a night manager meant being the last person standing, but I needed a challenge and persisted until he agreed.

Pilar visited Foxy's from time to time, in between auditions, before or after them.

"Karina, my friend I met in Miami in the acting world, and now lives in New York, is coming to visit. I want you to meet him. Can we come to Foxy's and eat?" Pilar asked.

"Of course!" I said, excited to have my friend visit as always.

Pilar walked in with her typical Cuban flair that lifts most spirits woken enough to take in the flavor. She reached over for a hug and was excited to introduce me to the tall, interesting character behind her.

"Karina, my friend Jerry!" Pilar said with the most innocent yet excited introduction.

"Hi, nice to meet you, Jerry!" I responded as I reached for a big hug and planted a kiss on his cheek. I'd learned from Pilar that hugs feel great and kisses on the cheek are ok when there's familiarity.

Jerry from South Jersey's response was colder than most while taken aback by my hug. He smiled and followed Pilar to the table.

"Are you guys hungry?" I asked.

They sat, enjoyed the meal and went about their outings for the weekend. These were the times Shan was talking about, the nights I'd wish to accompany my friends, the times I'd miss as a night manager.

Night shifts entailed a few unstable characters, one in particular who made the habit of sneaking through the front door when no one was looking, dialing 911 from the public phone next to the restrooms and sneaking out as quickly as he entered.

Sirens filled our parking lot with cops coming to an unnecessary rescue, leaving everyone wondering who had called 911. It took several times to catch his tall, lanky body and Speedy Gonzales pace as he walked in to the public phone and quickly walked out after dialing 911. It drove me nuts and pissed me off, while the waitresses and bus boys laughed.

We named him simply "Walkin-Walkout." He was slightly unstable but would be a blessing in disguise.

After a handful of false calls, the cops made the restaurant their coffee break stop and sometimes a place for dinner before or during their night shifts. I was familiar with the chief, a few detectives and several night shift cops who became good friends. When their nights were slow, they kept me company until 11 or midnight closings until the restaurant was ready for the next day while I tallied the till, also allowing the bus boys get a jump-start home. Thanks to Foxy's unstable "Walkin-Walkout," I learned lost angels also have messages and are blessings in disguise.

God uses us all for His purpose, even those unstable ones.

I learned about the cop world and the hard calls they have to make. I learned about their sacrifice and guarding because it's rare for them to answer happy calls. Every call is bound to be negative, violent and confrontational even though they always hope for a good resolution after gauging the scene and each person individually. I learned that every call could be their last and they do this for us, for the public. I learned to appreciate the police greatly and realized I could most certainly not marry one. It would be too much worry, particularly nowadays.

Life was somewhat smooth during my time at Foxy's. Pilar and I roomed well together; I had a structured schedule, and the partying slowed down, but life with Michael was either really fun or unbearably dysfunctional.

Michael had a good bottom line, but he carried a deep, wounded hurt and anger from the mother he rarely saw and yearned for. His hyper, erratic highs and lows were too much to take, leading me to break it off and add another one to the books. But not until he stalked me with endless demeaning and harassing calls and eventually got tired of getting on my roof trying to get inside my house. It was an act fitting for Michael, and one that my friends called "the roofer" after the time he spent on it stalking me.

When he finally stopped, I devoted myself to reading the bible and prayer time. I prayed and prayed for a nice, loving normal guy. I wondered if there was a normal guy with no mother issues, with principles and stability.

Be careful what you pray for, and pray specifically and carefully.

BE SPECIFIC IN YOUR PRAYERS AND HAVE FUN IN THE PROCESS

The words one uses in prayers are so important. The prayer, the need and intention should be more specific than the coffee orders I hear in Starbucks.

Michael was gone, and I was reminded of how to truly bring God into my life, with a deeper intention and connection than I was taught in my Catholic upbringing. I was beginning to take baby steps toward self-realization and healing, and now I was waiting for my prayer to be answered, for a normal, nice guy to come my way. In the meantime, I stumbled upon a mysterious bad boy with a motorcycle. Yes, it's pathetic and cliche.

Barry was edgy with attitude, dirty long hair and a walk to fit the look. But I think it was the stunning Harley-Davidson that I wanted to ride, particularly after I learned he was newly separated. So I took my time and focused on getting on the bike instead of the rebounding bad boy.

We became friends with boundaries set by me and often challenged by him. But when he surrendered to simply being friends, it was really fun as he showed me a taste of the motorcycle world. The ride was a treat.

Long rides on the Pacific Coast Highway and along those 27 miles of Malibu Oceanfront were exhilarating. We enjoyed an unspoken silence we quietly understood; we rode without a plan and stopped in holes-in-the wall for a bite to eat, eventually crossing over Kanan Road to the 101 Fwy and back home. But it was those dreaming, curvy roads along the mountains I fell in love with while looking back for a glimpse of the vast ocean as we headed east. The views are enormous and breathtaking. My favorite was somewhere in middle, the perfect spot offering the last of the ocean blessings and the first signs of the valley heat. There is something intriguing and mysterious about the drastic change of views, weather and lifestyle those mountains divide. I love them to this day.

Experiencing the tradition and loyalty among bikers was refreshing to see when I rode between thousands of bikes on the 55-mile trek from Glendale's Harley-Davidson's dealership to Castaic Lake for their annual Love Ride. The gear, community, cordiality, respect and responsibility bikers exhibited and shared were contrary to anything I knew of them.

I did pray for nice, but Barry was a rebel; he had a life he was separating from and a kid who would always be around. I was a kid myself, after all. He had more baggage than I had patience or ability to handle, and it was Pilar's friend who put it simply.

"Karina, you deserve the best. Find a guy you can start a fresh new life with. The bad boy thing will get old," said Armen.

I knew he spoke the truth, but it was the power of hearing it from a trusted source that moved me to cut ties with the rebellious bad boy with heavy baggage, possibly heavier than mine. It was hard and he was stubborn, eventually saying goodbye by breaking into my bedroom and dragging a Christmas tree into our living room as a goodbye gift.

Pilar was the first to see the bare tree plopped in the middle of the room and wondered why I had bothered to get one. She would be in Miami and I in Las Vegas for the holidays.

I didn't know where the tree had come from until Barry's goodbye call.

"Enjoy the Christmas tree. Every house should have one. And your bedroom window is unlocked. It's not safe for two pretty ladies," Barry stated somberly.

"Karina, where are my star and moon salt and pepper shakers?" Pilar shouted from the kitchen.

Barry overheard and responded: "Tell her to look at the top of the Christmas tree. They make great Christmas ornaments."

Goodbye, Barry.

Kel called out of the blue, excited for having met a guy she liked. One with a sports car, money and was also involved in the entertainment industry in some way or another. That was exciting for her. He also had a roommate she thought I should meet.

"He is so sweet, tall, utterly handsome and fit, and most importantly, he's not your typical LA guy, Karina. You must meet him," she shared with giggles while getting ready to hit the town with her new industry guy.

She was completely right. Scout was that and more. He was kind, centered, gentle, patient, compassionate and extremely considerate. He was my first taste of *normal*.

We spoke on the phone until wee hours of the night taking it moderately slow. We loved movies and spending lots of time together. He eventually moved in after he proposed.

I began to wonder if I had a "marry me" sign on my forehead considering this was my third engagement. I didn't understand the hurry to ask, but I always said yes because it always felt like the right thing to do. Had I said no, I'd have to find a reason, things to say. Yes was simpler.

Getting married seemed to be something I wanted, but it seemed so far-fetched, like a surreal necessary evil. Gloria rarely said much about my father, but when she did she vilified him and was suspicious of many others in her life. Her siblings didn't particularly exhibit happy, healthy marriages, and Alicia's husband left her and two kids for another woman, not to mention my own Gio, Kyle and Michael who lied, cheated and stalked. Marriage was not looking very appealing at all.

After Scout proposed and we moved into a small, darling house in the Hollywood Hills that he helped make a home with his art and touches of memories we were making, he began to gently suggest places to get married and a local bride dress location to visit. He also encouraged conversations with his family in Nebraska, who he was excited for me to meet and would probably attend the wedding.

I asked for this, I really did. I went to church, I prayed, I asked and God delivered. I asked for a nice, good guy. I was specific. God even threw me the looks, character and kindness, but I could not handle the possibility that I might actually deserve it. I had forgotten to pray for me, for my heart to heal from all that was boiling up inside. I forgot about me. I forgot to be more specific.

How could I have considered myself? There was absolutely

no way that Scout could care for me the way he did. I began to question his good deeds, love and affection and became unreasonably suspicious, like my mother, the woman I ran away from.

I often wonder what percentage of love we give and receive is a direct result of our upbringing. Do those with close to perfect childhoods give and receive close to perfect love? Can those like me change the cycle? Can we heal by doing the opposite? How do we learn that we're all deserving of goodness, kindness and respect? Is it self-awareness or accountability? Does it begin in the womb, or does it start with God? How and when do we change the cycle? Does it always have to be by hurting others and ourselves?

I prayed for it, I got it and I rejected it with fear, anger and rage. The poor guy didn't see it coming. The burst of rejection came without warning; it was literally out of left field. I took the long overdue bat and stuck him with it, an innocent bystander who had no idea what he had gotten himself into. He had no clue the baggage I had been carrying that was now exploding with full fury, bitterness and anger. It happened on his clock.

I wondered if Gloria and my father ever spoke of marriage. Gloria is typically not able to carry a serious conversation unless she's the victim in the story, so I can't imagine someone wanting to marry that frame of mind. But they had me, and the rest is a "what if" and "I wonder."

Besides my sweet, childless godparents who always displayed a loving partnership with actions and words, it was The Kinders' who showed me another version of marriage. An inclusive, fun and messy mix of two different forces, families and personalities trying to parent, work and be married with their own baggage.

Being truly loved, considered and compassionately cared for was deeply unfamiliar and uncomfortable. It was so foreign that I actually became angry, bitter and mean, mean to the bone. Scout didn't have a chance at all, the poor guy. The issue was me, and without any remorse or full understanding of the rage I felt, I gave him no explanation and kicked him out with all my might.

He could not console me or the situation. So he left quietly and smoothly after his sister reached out to plead for her brother:

"What's wrong with you? My brother is a really nice guy," she said after hearing a click.

He left when I was not there and left a book on anger and bitterness on my bed. The audacity, I thought as fumes crawled out of my skin feeling an immediate heat of anger at the ill-titled book. I was so blind. I'm so sorry, Scout.

Bottom line: always be specific like it's your last dying prayer or wish. Ask for yourself, your heart in the matter, and be super clear about what you want. Be careful what you wish for and make sure you're ready for what you're asking because I was not. I was not specific enough, and I often miss the mark and forget my heart's desire. I forget about me.

23

SINGLE WITH GOD

I've heard from some that "the Golden Rule" is a moral compass, their moral compass. The Golden Rule was given by Jesus of Nazareth, who used it to summarize the Torah: "Do to others what you want them to do to you. This is the meaning of the law of Moses and the teaching of the prophets," Matthew 7:12 NCV. So I believe the Golden Rule goes back to Christianity, to God.

My construed moral compass has been based on my Catholic upbringing. It was handed to me like rice and beans, tradition through and through, but a tradition that gave me a priest and an angelic loving nun, both of whom showered me with the order and consistency I greatly needed. The alternative was being handed off to others' lives and schedules. Without their knowing, or maybe with all of their knowing, my Catholic friends shaped my moral compass with shelter, love and guidance at a dire, young age when Gloria struggled to be a mother. They helped us both.

And while I consider the unfortunate, horrendous events the Catholic Church hides with dollar bills, I struggle knowing they also do great deeds. They cared when Gloria could not, as they cared for many others. This may be the reason I still crave and attend noon mini-masses from time to time, to calm the soul and reminisce about the good, while admitting I may have somewhat retired the imposed religion like many Catholics have. "Retired Catholics" is what I call us, yet we baptize our children because it's tradition, while keeping the religion itself at arm's length.

And while omitting the frowned-upon "organized religion" aspect God has been inevitably attached to, I love God, plain and simple.

I count on my walk, my relationship with Him. He, however, does not replace the figure of a loving and supportive physical father who was meant to give me unconditional love here on Earth. Not knowing my biological father has been an unfair burden that Gloria will never understand, and one I've had to carry on my own. Justifying the void of a parent is like discounting a part of one's heart and soul no matter what the excuse. *Two individuals* were needed to create me, a human being. The same were meant to raise me, a child; it's only common sense. And while applauding single parent heroes who are doing their best to fulfill two jobs, it isn't fair to the child and the double-duty parent. I know this first-hand. I know this now after raising a child of my own. It has been more than crystal clear to me that Kyra needs and requires her dad and me to play our individual roles in her life. It's not only a need, but a child's basic right.

My father may have been a chef, a great storyteller, an architect or a homeless being; it would not matter whatsoever, I'm sure of that. With matters of the heart, truth and honesty are the best nourishment setting an undeserved burden free. Even if the truth is sad, the sadness will be lifted by the truth itself. Truth is truth.

I had never walked with God the way I do now, after I met Pilar. Catholics do not traditionally read the bible or have a "relationship" the way Christian life does, and part of walking the Christian life is walking to bible study once a week, so I gave it a try.

When Pilar mentioned bible study, my curious mind pictured a classroom, a desk, a notebook, a pencil and a pastor who would recite the mighty book, much like a priest, but in more detail and without the Eucharist. On that weekday evening, I arrived at an apartment with no desk, notebook or pastor. The study began with hugs, kisses, loving conversations among each other and food, real food.

After everyone had their fill of chit-chat and catching up, a young, vivacious newlywed couple hosting the night opened the meeting with a detailed prayer that lasted longer than a traditional homily. The lengthy ask felt like a will. It went on and on. I wondered how long it would be, and I had never heard something so defined and detailed while all held hands and closed their eyes, though I kept one open. I wanted to see everything and everyone considering this was my first time at the rodeo.

When growing up, praying was a very private matter. And when praying next to Gloria, I often wondered if she was in pain when she prayed. Her eyes and hands were unusually tightly closed, praying hard enough that I could feel the strain in her body and frown on her face. It didn't make sense prayer should be that exhausting. I imagine she was praying for me, and for that I thank her always, but I wondered if she knew that God loves us no matter how hard the prayer and that He already knows our heart. I wondered if she knew prayer is an extension, a connection with Him, so why the strain? Just relax, He's listening.

After the long bible study opening will request, the host began the study by dissecting every line and verse, including the side notes in the bible that were not forgotten. They broke it apart to its very source, and I was fascinated, not at the bible initially, but at the level of study and attention paid in the room distracting me from the study itself. It was the humans who intrigued me. It was their surrendering to learning God's word, a much different commitment than my Catholic practice. It was foreign but refreshing.

Now that I was alone, after being the worst person I had ever been to a good human being, Scout, those long overdue, unresolved childhood issues came to the surface, one little memory at a time.

Still residing on a windy road in the Hollywood Hills, this was the first time I truly made an intention to live alone in my own space while filling up the darling house with my own trinkets and new beginnings.

We human beings think we know it all, that we can fix things with earthly solutions, some we can buy, some we create. At least that's what I thought, and that's what I did. I had a strong gut need to live alone, a crucial and required step to conquer before any other male crossed my path.

I needed to be in my own skin, with my own unraveling emotional junk that my body was excited to purge thinking it would bring me self-awareness, much-needed confidence and a sense of peace my heart was yearning for. But because my emotional baggage was not yet defined, and my desires were still on the surface, I did regular things to fill the time. I worked the hardest I have ever worked in my life. I exercised twice a day, read books and jogged endlessly around Lake Hollywood.

There was something very peaceful about that lake and the hills surrounding it. The comfort from the still water was shared by many who walked in front and behind me as we splattered pain and healed our way around the stillness.

At night alone, I watched classic black and white movies. Getting lost in Marlon Brando's pain was easy, while other nights I felt hopeful after Audrey Hepburn's emotional and gullible mess. But it was movies with relevant dialogue like *Guess Who's Coming to Dinner* or *My Man Godfrey* that kept me up all night. They were rich with content and character.

When my eyes were tired, my ears relished in my forever Bruce Springsteen singing about the common person's life and dreams or Alanis Morissette's angry, raw but refreshing lyrics that spoke to me and every other angry lost soul. She had a way of screaming my own pain and thoughts, while Fleetwood Mac taught me the beauty in poetry. It was a joint effort to set this girl free.

It's interesting what life brings when one is questing for goodness and healing with an open heart. I was indeed searching and open to change my imprint, to not repeat the cycle without really knowing how to do it. Yet, I knew deep in my heart that I was on to something different than I was given.

After months of gym sessions twice a day trying to gain health, body awareness and soothing myself with music, cardio and weights, an older gentleman took notice of my quiet existence floating through the gym.

Mark was open, happy and friendly from the moment he introduced himself. He walked with sophistication, knowledge and confidence fitting an attractive, fit, older man. We dined, hiked and watched movies, but it was awkward. I was just coming out of my shell barely making a crack, and he was older and wiser. We both felt the gap and ended our time together the most amicable way I had ever experienced. Maybe because he was a grownup.

In an effort to cross over as friends, we shared a last meal at a beautiful Italian restaurant where he'd share great wines to look for in the future and a few tips for life.

"Karina, never stop learning and take a 20-minute nap every day. It's good for the mind and health," Mark shared.

"Oookkkkay," I responded, knowing that the nap suggestion would be hard to follow.

"And I hope you don't mind the gift. I think you'll enjoy him and find it useful," Mark said as he handed me a box.

I must have been a real dud and an utterly boring human being. As a matter of fact, I know I was. I had absolutely no conversational skills, and he saw it. Although treading on thin ice, he gave me the entire collection of one of the best gifts anyone has ever given me, the classic Dale Carnegie, *How to Win Friends and Influence People,* packaged in the prettiest silver wrapping paper I had even seen.

It was indeed a gutsy gift at the time, leaning on the way of an insult, but when one is open and willing, one sees the opportunity and the upside, and that's what I did.

Dale Carnegie and Jim Rohn were in my ear every day for years ahead. They filled my mind at just the right time with the very information I didn't know I needed. My mighty Walkman went through piles of AA batteries, while my Ford Bronco rotated the fine tape to poor sound speakers, but it did not matter. I was a happy girl trying to catch up with life.

Soon after, and for some odd reason, a customer in the restaurant gifted me two very interesting books.

"Karina, here's some liberation," said the customer.

"Oh, Thank you," I responded and wondered what I needed liberation from, other than my childhood junk.

Naomi Wolf's *The Beauty Myth* and Gloria Steinem's *Revolution from Within* were handed to me.

Reading was never appealing to me as it is now, but I was hungry for knowledge and on a quest for doing new things, so I read Naomi and Gloria with an open mind, soon realizing their message was a drastic shift of information from Dale and Jim.

Before judging my customer on her choice of books, I wondered what it was in me that compelled her to hand me such particular dialogue. It may have been my sharing of spending a year alone to get myself straight realizing I may have forgotten to tell her that my year alone included God. Either way, Gloria Steinem and Naomi Wolf are indeed fascinating gals in their own right, only to be followed by their convictions and enlightening books riveting enough to consider my standing alone, and alone was the key word and my current state of events.

I was captured by both books, and because I had not been empowered by two loving parents, I was sucked into their world and empowered by their words, their views and perspective. Feminism seemed appealing and fitting for that year in my life. Feminism, a word I didn't know was a movement. How could I have known? But because I stumbled upon those books when I was single with God, the compelling movement was short lived, it felt strange.

I knew I needed to crawl out my skin and get comfortable with my shit, with my junk that will always be part of me but will not define me. I knew I needed movement, but for reasons I can't explain the feminist one seemed much like the space I was in, lonely and one sided. And as insecure as I was, and probably still am, I've always known I am worthy. I am a person of value with terribly flawed traits like everyone else. But just like everyone else, I need everyone else, and feminism felt lonesome because it seemed too individualistic. It seemed to omit a partner from the space I was reading from then and now.

When we are truly open and hungry for goodness, we receive nuggets of enlightenment splattered through our experience. The choice is ours to take, to savor each bite, and relish the nourishment it provides, or keep walking, doing the same thing with little to no results.

It was around this time I had an epiphany. I stumbled upon a very fitting book with a coincidentally appropriate title, at the local bookstore in downtown Burbank. "A Woman's Worth" radiated among the piles of books. It was not far from Gloria Steinem and Naomi Wolf's books. The title was inviting, and its pages were enough for me read over a weekend, except, it would not take me a weekend; it would take only one day to relish the beauty of Marianne Williamsons' words. I ate it up as if she was speaking my language and I would no longer feel crazy or alone. She spoke to my heart, enough so I attended an event where she was the speaker at the beautiful theater on Wilshire. Her dialogue was refreshing and riveting enough to compel me to invite Gloria, which I did on several occasions, in hopes she'd find self-worth of her own, in hopes she could realize that her worth was not in being my mother and placing that burden onto me, but that self-worth starts within, within our own hearts. I hoped that she could awaken, awaken to the realization that she is the owner of her own worth, but it failed, she couldn't conceptualize this ownership. Maybe because Marianne's dialogue went over her head, or there was too much to undo, too much to own or accept. Or, maybe because she was just tired and still is.

I kept trying, buying her books I liked, but the more I grew, the more estranged we became while leading different lives, with different aspirations, desires and accountabilities. I grew, she stayed put.

And that was that. Being single with God for that year brought me to my knees while running Lake Hollywood with tears of acknowledgement, forgiveness and acceptance for all good and bad in the past and the present, knowing that the future would be lighter and possibly brighter because God says so. It's that simple.

24

JERRY FROM SOUTH JERSEY

"Hi, Karina, it's me, Jerry Pacific, Pilar's friend from Miami. We met at Foxy's two years ago. I'm calling from New York."

It took some thought to put it all together. Two years ago is not last week, and Pilar never ever made a practice of sharing my contact information without asking me first. Most importantly, it's not like Jerry from South Jersey made a big impact on me after his cold and cautious hug. I had to dig deep and refresh my memory with no response.

"I hope you don't mind, but I called Pilar to ask for your contact. You were in my dream last night. Pilar also mentioned she's getting married in Miami and you'll be in the wedding. I lived in Miami for ten years. I'd be happy to pick you up and show you Miami like a local," Jerry from South Jersey carried on with no pause.

Many thoughts sped through my mind as he spoke. First, the fact that he wanted to show me Miami like a local after presuming my hug and kiss as being fresh and loose of me. Second, I wondered about the dream he had. It was probably sexual considering his loose thoughts. And third, I wasn't surprised I had made an impact on him. I was genuine, after all, joyous and just plain friendly, unlike him, who left a lot to be desired. Just saying.

As promised, Jerry picked me up at the airport driving a borrowed car, from his friend, the priest.

"Why did a priest lend you his car?" I asked.

"He was my priest when I lived here in Miami and is a dear friend. He's out of town and lent me his car."

Jerry from South Jersey may not be so bad after all. I could relate to being friends with a priest and nun, and it was refreshing he had faith, unlike the three numbnuts I had dated. Jerry began to look all right.

He shared his concern for me and the wedding party due to recent Miami airport kidnappings. My inside voice said, Sure, Jerry from South Jersey, whatever you need to tell yourself.

Jerry did follow through with the best tour of Miami while exploring it like a local, the best way to see any city as far as I'm concerned. All I had to do was relax, eat, sightsee, drink and repeat.

Miami has a particular flavor and dance in the air. I felt it the moment I got off the plane. The air is humid and flavorful, and the streets are filled with culture and passion, particularly during every conversation I encountered. It's a blast.

Jerry made a habit of arriving every morning to the hotel we all stayed in with a tray full of Cuban *coladas*.

A *colada* is Cuban espresso served in a Styrofoam cup meant to be shared and a customary drink in the Cuban community. It's a nice gesture, and one that would probably redeem Jerry from two years ago. Apart from the obligatory bridesmaids' appointments, Jerry made himself available to us all.

Miami is where he moved from South Jersey with his high school girlfriend and her family, he told me, and when the invite presented itself, he left his roots and parents. The story felt familiar. After he and his Jersey girl parted ways, he was on his own to fend for himself in a city with a different pulse, a different language and culture enough to think it was Havana itself.

He took us shopping through Coconut Grove during humid days and ten-minute spurts of rain, common for Miami, the locals said. We drove through Coral Gables and the streets he lived on as he shared all about surviving Hurricane Andrew. Jerry's storytelling painted a vivid visual of a rented room behind a house whose owners were out of town when Andrew began to show himself with winds and furious rain. Jerry had been briefed how to handle the house in case of a hurricane, and it occurred to me that I probably would not be able to handle a large earthquake in Los Angeles alone, even though I had lived through the Northridge quake.

How does one prepare for gushing winds lifting trees and cars, tearing through homes with no mercy in sight? What does one do when the ground shakes and is angry enough to break underneath us, cutting through our lives? Mother nature shows up in every town, and I must prepare myself when I get home, I promised myself.

Jerry had little time to move through the massive house making sure all protective shutters were securely locked enough to keep Andrew out. Time stood still.

Gray stillness, bent streetlights, fallen street signs, and wet despair changed Miami. Andrew came, went and left an unprecedented mess behind. But the moments of truth were the first times Jerry drove through his neighborhood. What neighborhood? he wondered. The trees and signs he relied on were gone. Where is my left and right? It was one lush, wet mess.

After spending a handful of days and nights with the Jersey boy, it was during the rehearsal dinner that I realized I was in trouble, that I was basically fucked.

People were celebrating the upcoming union of Pilar and David.

Delicious Cuban and Mexican food filled everyone's plates. Someone was always dancing and drinking perfectly made mojitos only Miami knows how to do. It was heaven. Latinos party with the love and passion we were born with. I was in a beautiful room filled with Cubans and Mexicans. Life was good, and I was out of my mind happy soaking in both cultures and friends, until Pilar got a glimpse of me.

She approached me as deliberately as the first time I met her.

"What's wrong with you?" She asked looking straight at me with her big, brown, intense stare so typical when she wants truth, and nothing but the truth.

"Are you drunk?" she continued, wanting a response.

"No, well, maybe. I'm fucked, that's what I am. I've fallen in love."

"With whom?" she asked.

"Jerry, your friend, of course," I laughed. "Who else?" And I ran off to dance before she could say a thing. The night was slipping by.

During my time being Single with God, while listening to music and writing, I began to write a small bucket list. One courageous and slightly scary item was to take a trip by myself, to explore a new place alone, and what better place than the Bahamas?

"You're nuts. Don't do it. It's dangerous," my dear friend Erik pleaded.

"YOU'RE nuts! You don't leave your own bubble enough to have an opinion," I responded and hung up.

I took Erik's concern and invited Jerry to accompany me, only to receive a decline.

It seemed fitting at the time. The Bahamas was a breath away from Miami. I knew I needed to do it before life interrupted me with other useless distractions.

Pilar married one the best individuals I've ever known. Festivities were over. Jerry headed back to New York to pack and then head to Los Angeles, and I escaped to paradise.

It took my breath away. The Bahamas do that. There are no words to describe the beautiful waters and warmth. And as stunning as it was, it was overkill. The Nassau Atlantis Resort that was new at the time was safe and beautiful, but it was massive and felt lonely for a single girl traveling alone.

I made the best of it, taking advantage of all activities offered. I slept in every morning, walked the entire resort several times and gambled a bit. Dinner and nighttime were lonely, and this is when Erik called to make sure I was ok and alive while reprimanding me for being alone in a foreign country. He was mainly perplexed as to why Jerry had declined my invitation to the Bahamas.

"He's gay," Erik said. "How does a straight man decline three overnights with you? He's gay." I ignored him and continued talk about his day in the bubble he never leaves, the valley.

Jerry from South Jersey moved to Miami, then to New York and finally arrived in the City of Angels. The guy covered three corners of the nation. Pretty cool, I thought.

Upon his arrival and after settling in, I showed him Los Angeles like a local, like an Angeleno of course, with pride and joy, joy he rarely shared. His East Coast sensibility clashed with my beloved La La angel city, a love-hate sentiment most East Coasters share about Los Angeles, one he had no problem exhibiting. He complained about traffic, confusing freeways and Santa Ana winds as he sneezed his way through more complaints. He swore only people in LA were late. He grumbled about the superficial entertainment industry. He complained about the lack of good theatre. You name it, he complained about it.

His comical curmudgeonly and endearing approach was always funny and quick-witted softened by those Pacific droopy eyes. Sarcastic East Coast jabs about common things always made sense, and every frustration ended with "This is ridiculous," as he walked away trying to make sense of my beloved Los Angeles.

This would be my training for most things East Coast, and although it brought me honest comedy and belly laughs, it would also bring tension in the air many years later.

Realizing I had failed miserably at relationships up until this time, I found myself approaching Jerry much differently than the other birdbrains I had chosen in the past.

It was now important for me to acknowledge that I and only I had picked the knuckleheads who asked me to marry them, and because I picked them and I recognize it, it was important for me to also understand why I chose them, in hopes these decisions would help me break the pattern. In choosing Jerry, whether good or bad, it was a conscientious choice, one that I had to be accountable for.

As Jerry and I began to spend days and nights together, it was clear we were onto something. We were both raised Catholic, and we enjoyed the evolving world of wellness. I honestly would not have minded if he was Christian or Jewish; faith in God in particular was now important after the numbnuts in the past, and it would prove to be instrumental in our lives ahead.

His sense of humor is important and one of the main reasons we are still together. His blunt, sarcastic, free-thinking common sense has also helped me rethink the way I had shaped things in my head. He has a way of calling discernment in times when it's needed, in times when we actively make choices to be ok with the status quo. Yes, as fun as it was, I began to realize that underneath it all, he also came with pain and sadness hidden in the comedy because that is the source of comedy, emotional pain and baggage bundled in a joke. Since I had already made strides with some of my own, I began to see the signs but ignored them with laughter.

Growing up in Mexico was typically by the ocean, just short of two miles away from the prettiest beach lined with straw umbrellas and colorful chairs on the beach. In America, however, I had lived "inland" having to scratch my ocean need by heading to Malibu and Santa Monica every weekend for jogs, bike rides and stair workouts in the popular stair trails of San Vicente. Jerry also gravitated to the blue water after years of being raised in Ocean City, New Jersey, every summer. In an effort to relieve his ongoing Santa Ana wind misery, we began to head to South Bay.

We went to the beach every weekend starting with Sunday Mass as his weekly ritual, a ritual I believed was more flexible than he practiced. Sometimes Mass is sitting quiet in prayer at the bus stop, while waiting for food or by attending nondenominational service. But, no, Mass is Mass, he'd say, so I followed knowing full well God walks with us every step and missing one Mass will not warrant a flash through the sky.

West Hollywood's "Saint Victor's" or Santa Monica's "Saint Monica" were our eulogies of choice followed with breakfast in the same pancake house every time we entered Manhattan Beach from Vista Del Mar while enjoying the stretch of the Pacific. Uncle Bill's was a weekly stop after the first visit. Jerry fell in love with the quaint beach feel and breakfast counter in the darling pancake house where he made friends with the owner who shared a love for cigars.

After many calorie-filled pancakes later, Jerry was referred to a job in a local cigar club, appropriately so. And that was that, my single time with God officially ended. My relationship with God continued and grew, but with a Jersey boy at my side. Any more healing from it all now had to be done next to him, Jerry, who had his own issues I sensed yet ignored. It couldn't be as bad as the numbnuts I had invited in the past, I thought. Going in, I was realistic. I knew he wasn't perfect. Who doesn't have baggage? I justified to myself. Who meets, falls for and marries a completely flawless partner? I wanted to know. And when no one spoke, I moved to South Bay with the newfound Jersey boy.

As for Gloria during this time, we shared birthdays and visits from time to time. The more time passed, the more distant we grew...I grew. I began to feel as though we were strangers, and to some degree we are, something I've also had to forgive.

I often think about God and His perfect plan to place me in front of Pilar who brought me back to Him, to God Himself, when I was lost, tired and torn down without knowing it. What if I had not hiked those Burbank hills that day, which led me to that particular liquor store picking up the last newspaper looking for a place to live? Would I have ever been found in such a significant way at Emmanuel Church? Would I have met Jerry and now have a miracle, my Kyra?

What about His dream I played in? I refuse to think it's all a coincidence. It's too simple to say, when in all reality, it's Him. It's always God working His loving magic.

And so it begins, a life with a funny curmudgeon. A life we'd have to grow up in together, on our own, to do marriage the way it was never taught to us.

25

DROPPING LIKE FLIES

#1 RUFELIO

"Hello," I said.

"Hola Kari, ¿cómo estás?"
"Hi, Kari, how are you?" Gloria asked.

"Bien, gracias, ¿y usted?"
"Good, thank you, and you?" I responded wondering if I should have asked.

"Más o menos, bueno, Rufelio murió. ¿Te acuerdas de él? Él era muy bueno."
"Ay, ay, ay, well, Rufelio died. Do you remember him? He was very nice."

"Oh, lo siento. No, no me acuerdo de él. Cuídese."
"Oh, I'm sorry. No, I do not remember him. Take care of yourself."

"Ay, Kari, tú no te acuerdas de nadie. Él te compró una blusa cuando eras niña."
"Ay, Kari, you don't remember anyone. He bought you a shirt when you were little," she responded with a frustrated tone thinking I should remember Rufelio's gesture when I was little.

"Es triste que haya muerto, pero, ¿cómo quiere que yo recuerde a alguien que me dio una blusa cuando yo era niña?"
"It's sad that he died, but how could I remember someone who gave me shirt when I was little?"

"Ay, Karina, ¿cómo es posible que seas así? Adiós."
"Ay, Karina, how is it that you are the way you are? Bye."

#2 SEÑORA MARÍA

"Hello."

"Hola, Kari, ¿cómo estás?"
"Hi, Kari, how are you?" Gloria asks.

"Bien, gracias, ¿y usted?"
"Good, thank you, and you?" I responded wondering if I should have asked, like I usually do.

"Ay, ay, ay, bueno, la Señora María murió. ¿Te acuerdas de ella? Ella era muy buena."
"Ay, ay, ay, well, Señora Maria died. Do you remember her? She was very nice."

"Oh, lo siento. No, no me acuerdo de ella. Cuídese."
"Oh, sorry. No, I do not remember her. Take care of yourself."

"Ay, Kari, tú no te acuerdas de nadie. Ella nos hacía comida cuando yo trabajaba tarde."
"Ay, Kari, you don't remember anyone. She made us food when I worked late."

She responded with judgment for my not remembering one of

the hundreds of individuals who fed us when she worked late, which was often when I was little, may I add.

"Es triste que haya muerto, pero, ¿cómo quiere que yo recuerde alguien que nos dio comida cuando usted trabajaba hasta tarde y yo era chica."
"It's sad that she died, but how could I remember someone who gave us food when you worked late when I was little?"

"Ay, Karina, ¿cómo puedes ser así?. Adiós."
"Ay, Karina, how is it that you are the way you are? Bye."

Calls like these continued on a monthly basis. She must have gone through ten dead people who did or gave something when I was little, people I should remember because the deed was so big in a time she needed it, but I was too little to remember.

#UMPTEENTH DEATH

"Hello."

"Hola, Kari, ¿cómo estás?"
"Hi, Kari, how are you?" Gloria asked.

"Bien gracias, y usted?"
"Good, thank you, and you?" Regretful to ask based on her growing trend.

"Ay, ay, ay, bueno, mi hermano, tu Tío José se murió. ¿Te acuerdas de él? Él era muy bueno, me ayudó y te cuidaba mucho. ¡Él te quería tanto!"

"Ay, ay, ay, well, my brother, your Uncle Jose, died. Do you remember him? He was very nice. He helped me and used to take care of you a lot. He loved you very much."

"SÍ, SÍ, ¡CLARO QUE LO RECUERDO BIEN!"

I responded with conflicted excitement to finally know one of these dead souls, quickly realizing I actually felt his death deeply. I remembered him the most as we bar hopped and walked my neighborhood making quiet conversation, with his six-pack and cigarettes at hand. He may have had his vices, but he was gentle, kind and took care of me as often as he could.

I continued, *"Yo me acuerdo muy bien de él. Tengo lindas memorias suyas. Eso sí es triste. Mami, finalmente alguien quien conozco. Estaba empezando a pensar que la gente que se sigue muriendo eran fantasmas. Mami, su gente en México se está cayendo como moscas. ¿Qué está pasando allá?"*
"YES, YES, OF COURSE I remember him well. I hold dear memories of him. That is very sad. Mami, finally someone I know who died. I began to think these people dying were ghosts. Mami, your people in Mexico are dropping like flies. What's going on over there?"

"KARINA, ¿cómo me preguntas eso? ¿Por qué eres así?"
"KARINA, how do you ask a question like that? Why are you like that?"

"Mami, siempre que me llama, alguien se muere, van diez personas más o menos, y solamente una que yo conocí. Yo no entiendo esta situación, pero ¡por Dios! ¿Qué está pasando?"
"Mami, every time you call me, someone has died, ten people give or take, and only one person I know. I don't understand the situation, but my God, what's happening?"

"Ay, Karina, ¿cómo es posible que seas así. Adios."
"Ay, Karina, how is it that you are the way you are? Bye."

Our conversations and connection after I left her, after high school, were always on the surface. How are you? Great. Be careful. God bless you, etc. Gloria rarely knew about my whereabouts, my travels, where I was resting my head for the night or what numbnut I was dating. Conversations and dialogue rarely occurred, and when they did, she did not know how to digest the vast difference between us. And I, well, I was exploring life beyond her comprehension.

But it was the morbid, depressing phone calls that began to take a toll on the connection we were hanging onto. I was hoping to read something into them, a clue from every death call wondering if she herself was dying even when she said she was not, or was she watching too many Mexican novelas, or was she asking for love and attention in all the wrong ways? But after many calls of people dropping like flies and my trying hard to get clues, "Why the outcry? What is she really asking for with all of these deaths?" the result only caused more separation between us, leaving me wondering if she had any clue what she was ultimately doing.

My concern was how my heart was being shaped about death. She began to make it sound so morbid, like the Sunday news, but it was the expectations she placed on me. She expected me to feel the way she did about death, things and people I didn't know, and that's when I began to create boundaries.

#LAST VICTIM

"Hello."

"Hola, Kari, ¿cómo estás?"
"Hi, Kari, how are you?" Gloria asked, somber as always.

"Bien gracias, ¿y usted?"
"Good, thank you, and you?" I responded knowing I may snap if someone else had died.

"Ay, ay, ay, bueno, la señora Luz se murió. ¿Te acuerdas de ella?"
"Ay, ay, ay, well, Mrs. Luz died. Do you remember her?"

With all the patience and kindness I could muster, I calmly responded:

"Mami, ya no puedes llamarme porque alguien se murió. Tampoco puedes esperar que a mí me duela como te duele a tí. Yo no los conozco, y más que nada, no entiendo cómo es que conoces tantas personas que mueren, irónicamente tan cerca

uno del otro, y a quienes nunca he conocido, y si los hubiera conocido, habría sido cuando era muy joven, posiblemente en mi infancia. Así que perdóneme por no saber quiénes demonios eran esas almas perdidas. Obviamente no fueron suficientemente importantes en mi vida para que yo lo recuerde. Por favor, te lo suplico, necesitas romper este hábito de dolor y malas noticias. Solo puedes llamarme cuando tengas buenas noticias y cualquier cosa positiva en tu vida. Tal vez, por ejemplo, si alguien que tu conozcas tuvo un bebé, un nuevo nacimiento para reemplazar uno de los tantos muertos de tu lista."

"Mami, you are no longer allowed to call me about someone else dying. You are also not allowed to expect me to hurt like you hurt. I do not know them. I mainly don't understand how you happen to know so many people who are ironically dying so close together AND whom I may not have met, and if I had met them, it would have been when I was very young, possibly infancy. So forgive me for not knowing who the hell these dying souls were. Please, I plead for you to break this habit of need for sorrow and bad news. You're only allowed to call me with good news and anything positive in your life. Maybe, just maybe, someone you know had a baby, a new fresh birth to replace one of the many dead ones from your list."

Gloria responded with her typical how-dare-you response, *"KAARRIIINAAAAA! ¿Cómo pudiste?... ¿cómo te atreves?"*
"How could you? How dare you?"

"Gloria, dime algo positivo. Llámame con algo positivo. Tú puedes, inténtalo."
"Gloria, tell me something positive. Call me with something positive. You can do it, try."

"No me llames Gloria, soy tu madre."
"Don't call me Gloria, I'm your mother." She hung up.

But Gloria is what she became the weekend I left, the weekend I chose to raise myself, the same weekend she let me, never knowing what I was up to. I became the adult and she stayed put.

After I ended those morbid calls is when our relationship shifted. Like longtime friends and one decides to grow up. That twist in everyone's dynamic when lines are drawn and one party is bound to feel hurt and wronged. That was the time I raised boundaries yearning for a healthy, positive relationship, not to punish her or take her for granted for all that she was able to do, but because I wanted more from her emotionally, but she just couldn't. I wanted her to walk the walk of the faith she claimed.

Back home, in Mexico, ironically and fitting for Gloria's proclivity, I did enjoy our monthly travel to and time in the cemetery. From my eyes, it was one big, mysterious playground.

The bus ride was quiet and long, much like driving on the 15 FWY on the way to Las Vegas.

Gloria's mother had died when she was young, and she never mentioned her father. Maybe that's the reason she avoided conversations about mine. Our main mission was my grandmother's tombstone on those hot Sunday visits, and that's what she focused on. I, on the other hand, explored as I typically did.

Flowers, rags and a broom were carried in the bus to sweep and dust around her deceased mother. Once settled and the quietness set in, I quickly dusted off my grandmother's real estate to move on to other interesting plots and visit other souls in the neighborhood.

Burial plots varied drastically from one to the other. Engraving and details about each ranged enough to envision the life and family they left behind. It was an interesting mix of designs, stones, sentiments, flowers and dust. Details that kept me moving from one to another.

It was the only space where there was no class division. The poor and rich were all mixed up, all in one, and it was the rich who received the least amount of visits exhibited by the dust and dead leaves on those plots.

I dusted off any plot that grabbed my attention while respectfully settling into their space, sometimes feeling their energy by particular breezes that moved through me.

Besides the beautiful, colorful decorations and flowers Mexican cemeteries are adorned with, it was the spontaneous energy, calm and mystery it offered giving me great clarity about my space, our space in this world. That we are all human beings who have the honor to make daily choices to live life fully or to survive life with excuses. The choice is ours until that one day when we end up six feet under.

Gloria arranged her plot and paperwork decades ago, while a dear friend calls me periodically to discuss his fear of death, what he's left behind for his kids and feeling of missing out. And while I listen to his concerns while alive, and ponder Gloria's relationship with death, I wonder if they've spent the same effort on enjoying the life above ground as they do about death.

It was the small, private mausoleums that intrigued me, curiosity that urged me to open their gates and explore the mystery a little bit closer. Why the big casita when the soul is underground and its neighbor was barely covered by dirt that became mud when it rained?

Maybe this is why Gloria took care of her burial business twenty years ago, so her death will be done her way.

As a result, *Dia de los Muertos* has become one of my favorite Mexican celebrations. A tradition intended to *celebrate* those who have departed, not *sorrow*. And that's what I chose to do, to celebrate those who passed with gratitude for their presence, as opposed to dramatizing the life like a Mexican *novela,* Gloria's way.

My way is a positive way. I'm not worried about the pain from the past, age or death. I'm worried about missing life and its beauty. Have I done what I was here to do? Will my soul remain, or will it have cycled enough to be truly put to rest? I'll never know. I do know cemeteries are not scary. They are all full of souls and wisdom if you stand still enough to celebrate their lives because we're all worthy of being celebrated, dead or alive.

I love Gloria, my mother, my courageous, stubborn as a bull, tenacious and resourceful mother. As much as I applaud her, I fell short of the emotional mother-daughter relationship we could have had, but she couldn't do it, maybe because she wasn't given what I needed, but she chose not to try.

And that's the lesson, that we have the power of acceptance and choice. We choose to do or not based on our hurt, ego and fear, and she let them all take over goodness and love. The more I forgive her journey, her will and choices, the more I understand my actions and those around me.

Oh my sweet little girl, Gloria, I hope one day you let love and be love.

26

CHANGING THE MOTHER SIGNATURE IN MARRIAGE

There is something endearing about those East Coast characters who have an edge intense enough to wake a pulse, an edge they can't seem to round themselves, but their charm is distracting enough to make you forget you're now sharing the same energy because there is some truth in the matter.

I have yet to figure out where that edge comes from. La La is too la la to bother with the intensity the East Coast derives. We're too chill for it. We have too much sunshine, more vitamin D than our body requires. We have too many miles of Pacific Coast to contemplate our navels with "what if's" and soothing warm weather to make us forget seasons exist in a state filled with more changing blue liberations than we know what to do with.

The East Coast edge may begin with the cold weather and snow, or the many states compacted together in that little Northeast corner where America's history was inked by its founding fathers, the same history our schools are trying to sugar coat, yet, utilize. Maybe it's that edge.

It was a lazy Sunday in my Melrose Place-like apartment complex where a Mexican girl and an Italian Jersey boy sealed the deal with a kiss.

The Sopranos kept us in for a day of binge watching trying to catch up with everyone's TV show addiction.

Jerry fixed us a couple of delicious Cadillac Margaritas while I finished mixing the perfect guacamole and chips. We set up shop on the floor and leaned against layers of pillows perfectly set for hours of riveting, intriguing watching.

"Wait, I love him. Wait, I didn't know he was an actor," I said, but not really. I knew it was Little Steven missing his trademark bandana.

"Wait, he has hair, or is it fake?"

"How do you know Little Steven?" Jerry asked.

"I'm a huge fan of The Boss and his E Street Band. It's a long story. Little Steven is good!" I responded, excited to get a version of the E Street Band in my living room, unaware of Jerry's personal moment, until he reached over to plant his first kiss.

After a few minutes of tongue twisting and feeling his luscious lips, I pulled back.

"Why the sudden kiss?"

It was out of the blue. I was taken aback. After all, he hadn't made any moves in quite some time making me wonder if Erik was right. "He's gay, Karina."

"I can't believe you like Bruce Springsteen and the E Street Band. He's one of my favorites, and he's from New Jersey," Jerry shared.

"Oh, well of course I know he's from New Jersey!"

And that was that. It would take me liking The Boss, a commonality of such for Jerry to make his move. After a little more tongue twisting, we went back to *The Sopranos,* and he and I were officially a thing.

Jerry and I began to visit his hometown in South Jersey several times a year. He took enormous pride and joy in sharing his love for the Jersey shore he grew up in, Ocean City in particular. He shared each shop, ride and eatery like a boy sharing his beloved train set.

The Ocean City Boardwalk indeed elicited a playfulness that even the grumpiest of East Coasters were forced to grin and enjoy.

The Boardwalk shared by my New Jersey boy brought a lightness and gentle childness Jerry shows on a need-to-know basis. They come few and far between.

"Ocean City is a dry town after we cross the little bridge," Jerry informed me in what felt like a warning.

I was perplexed considering the Atlantic Ocean was on the other side of the bridge, and stores sold water. Ocean City didn't seem to be dry to me.

It became a tradition to dine during each visit at the Crab Shack with any member of the Pacific crew in town. The Crab Shack is a spacious restaurant just before the bridge, and one that could sit our big group for their delicious oversized seaside meals and their popular Crab Imperial plate, the favorite of Jerry's and Jeff's (Jerry's brother).

How was the Boardwalk? My soon-to-be sister-in-law Terry asked.

"Pretty and very different from our beach communities in SoCal," I responded.

"You can drink in your beach towns, though. Ocean City has always been dry. You probably need a drink after all that walking," Terry continued.

"I drank water. It's not dry," I responded and continued being confused why they felt their beach town didn't sell liquids.

Gentle laughs filled the loud restaurant and table, as Jerry leaned over to inform me that a dry town is a town that does not sell alcohol.

I laughed; we all laughed. I did think it was interesting and praiseworthy that there are still a few "dry" towns in America, particularly when the larger demographic that visits is under age.

The Ocean City Boardwalk is indeed a must-see. The shore is a piece of old-school seaside nostalgia adored with uniquely placed wood planks to walk over. A sentimental feel that creates memories along the way when walking on it and passing through the pizza joint, arcade or saltwater taffy stores that have been there for decades.

It would be on the Ocean City Boardwalk next to a bench that Jerry would get on his knees for me to be his bride, with a Fudge Candy box to seal the deal because the ring was not quite ready and he didn't want to miss the moment.

Like the kiss, it was out of the blue, and like the kiss, I went for it with a Yes!

Jerry is the youngest of four boys, four good men. Danny, Bob, Jeff and Jerry in that order, sons of the sweet Fred and Joyce, the mother.

After much observation and several summers and holiday visits to the Jersey shore staying with Jeff and Terry, I was able to enjoy the dynamic of all the brothers who are uniquely different and comical, with Jerry being a blend of all, sharing a commonality or two from each of his eldest brothers.

Jerry's upbringing was much like the typical all-American childhood I've read about, seen on movies and shows. He thought so, and he wore it almost like a badge. If there is such a thing as the all-American upbringing, his would have been it as far as he was concerned. I would have agreed, but not until the matriarch showed her colors.

He was raised by the loving, hardworking and kind Fred. Fred was of Italian descent. He took the train to work in Philadelphia every day to feed his family of six. He never drove, and although I met him after he had retired, he never complained. I imagine that was his nature all of his life. He might not have shown his boys how to play baseball or shown them the mechanics of a car, but he did offer a loving, calming nature and an insatiable laugh Jerry can easily replicate.

Joyce, oh Joyce. She was a wife and mother who made every meal for all while keeping the house moving. She also had a voice and temperament not to be reckoned with.

Blue-eyed Danny is the eldest. He shares a natural flow for storytelling with comedic common sense, much like Jerry. Danny lays out stories about the blue collar, working middle class in New Jersey he is part of, while enjoying a love for his three close-to-perfect boys, grown men now, and his wife, Cathy. Danny loves history, food, good wine and a great cigar.

Bob the builder, the quiet one who lives in the woods, and who makes a practice of building his homes with his own two hands. Bob is a smart, introverted fella married to Janice, also sweet and introverted, a perfect match. Bob the builder comes with a wine and coffee snob approach he makes no excuses for, and a handiness I admire and envy.

Jeff, oh that silly Jeff. They broke the mold with him. Jeff is one of a kind. He is wicked smart, quick-witted, artistically gifted and one of the most comically animated storytellers I have met. I have always been fascinated by this modest fella who tells thoroughly descriptive plots filled with physical gestures, voiceovers, mannerisms and non-politically correct common sense content making anyone laugh, even the stiffest one in the room. Jeff has three healthy kids, grandkids and one spicy redheaded Italian wife who loves big and graciously shares her home as if it was your own during every visit.

All of the Pacific men are good men. They are handsome with Fred's best features, his kindness, height and good looks. They have integrity, a work ethic and charm.

After many mistakes, obliviousness and numbnuts in the past, I wanted to go deeper with relationships. I wanted to know Jerry's bottom line, and that meant getting to know the family's core, later to realize the core began with Joyce, the mother, quickly realizing it most always begins with the mother. A great epiphany as far as relationships go, and one I'll have to be accountable for as a mother myself.

It took much time and many visits with his family in New Jersey while celebrating birthdays, summers and holidays that I realized the little gut feeling I had ignored with laughter was now rearing its ugly head the closer I looked, and the more I observed Joyce.

The more memories I began to create in New Jersey, the more acquainted Joyce and I became. And although we lived 3,000 miles away from her, and Jerry and I now married with a child, I wanted my daughter, Kyra, now a toddler, to enjoy her East Coast family, her sweet aunties and cousins she had been born into as much as we could visit.

Summer barbeques, days at the shore, day trips to Philadelphia for history recaps or Cape May afternoons, my favorite little town, all became a norm. Traditions and memories created jam-packed photo albums for Kyra's sake, until I began to see a disturbing trend.

Joyce was a force most did not challenge. She made herself heard with loving grandmother gestures only to be followed with ill motherless remarks to Jerry, my husband, the father of my offspring. The jabs were subdued, underhanded and demeaning more often than not. It was the insulting personal profanities that felt like a knife in my stomach, and I could not imagine how they felt to Jerry. I knew I had my own set of family issues, but no one had ever spoken to me the way Joyce spoke to her son. I then realized she was the genesis, that little gut feeling that was off about Jerry, the gut feeling I ignored with laughter.

After some time while finding myself colluding with the dysfunctional space Joyce created with Jerry in front of Kyra, the momma bear in me crawled out to defend my family while treading on thin ice when I decided to burst Jerry's bubble about his "all-American childhood."

"Jerry, I may have had an emotionally absent mother, and lacked a father, but one thing I know for sure, mothers are supposed to nurture. Mothers are not supposed to talk to their sons like your mother does to you. I'm sorry."

I repeated the sad sentiment with what I felt was a loving, compassionate approach, while nervous to judge his mother hen. He would not respond again.

He did stare into my eyes with deep sadness, with those sweet Italian Fred eyes all the Pacific men share. I didn't need to be right; I needed him to know that unkind words are not ok from anyone, most particularly our parents.

"Jerry, I do not want Kyra to hear her grandmother, your mother, speak to you the way she does. It's not nice. She's not nice, I'm sorry."

I was actually thinking of Joyce as well, I really was, I swear. I wanted to keep Kyra from any negative memories of a mean- spirited grandmother. I was trying to keep any good memories there were about Joyce intact.

Still no response from my Jersey boy, just a pair of solemn eyes in deep thought of a reality he might have known but ignored. His mind was gone, maybe thinking about the fact that he had passed judgment on his wife's unorthodox upbringing, only to realize I was now pulling the rug from under his all-American one, or so he thought. Or the fact that he knew it all along and could no longer ignore it having a child himself. I tried to read him, but his silence filled our space with the profound sorrow it deserved. And when I felt his pain, I went to work.

After several trips, the energy began to shift in him when she was in the room, particularly after a mouthful of dismissive, underhanded comments directed at him. He changed; innocent bystanders in the room changed; our relationship changed. Above all, Kyra changed by feeling the energy, and that's when it got personal.

During what were supposed to be fun, memory-filled trips, I began to challenge Joyce to be kinder, to speak with positive words or to simply omit negative ones for that matter. After much effort, it was clear she was too old to change, that her antagonistic, malevolent character traits I was working against had their own pain and sorrow. Unfortunately at the time, I could not sympathize or help her. I had a family to protect.

"Joyce, that's not nice. He's your son. Please don't speak to him like that," I pleaded with calmness and patience, while my inside voice, the Latina in me, was going off in Spanish.

"Joyce, please don't speak to Jerry with insulting words. Kyra is watching you." She dismissed me with a smile and jabs intended to be funny, but they never were.

This is when I knew there was absolutely no chance I could have a positive impact in the situation. If I couldn't do it with my own mother, I certainly was not going to be successful with a tough, grown Philly girl.

"Jerry, Gloria lacked nurturing and mothering, but she never disrespected me or called me unkind names. I don't know, Jerry, but I don't think you had the all-American upbringing you have been claiming. I don't want Kyra around this. I'm sorry."

And that was that. He said, "Ok," and the visits to the East Coast took a sharp turn.

Months after creating boundaries to make the best of our relationship with Joyce, I was surprised to find myself grieving the wish I had for her and me. I had looked forward to learning from her, to her stories of raising four rambunctious boys. I imagined that was a lot of work. I had looked forward to the "back in the day" stories wise people love to share or family recipes for me to try and hand over to Kyra for her own family. Instead, I found myself switching gears I never thought I had to use, gears to protect my family from any negative influence she may have had on us as long as she lived. The problem was, Joyce much like Gloria, had already influenced our family, leaving us to maneuver their good and wrongdoing, their mother signature.

As for Jerry, I skated through that conversation better than I thought. Not that I worried, my concern was my child, and the anger Jerry must have been bottling in for quite some time, the same anger I would have to deal with sooner or later. I was after all criticizing his mother, the human being who put him on Earth, and by the grace of God, Jerry understood my concern for him, but mainly Kyra. It was a chance I was willing to take because Jerry and I often looked eye-to-eye on the way we wanted to raise Kyra, and our mothers' way was clearly not our way.

Fred left us with the same calm nature I knew him to have. I should have attended his funeral. Maybe I was scared of those unfamiliar feelings funerals elicit. He was the first funeral sendoff I truly felt sad about. He was a wonderful father, loving grandfather and beautiful soul to me. I wanted to leave it at that. And maybe I also didn't want to see Joyce. I didn't want her energy overshadowing the sweet Fred memories I still have to this day. He knows where my heart is; he's shown me from time to time.

As for Joyce, she passed a few years after, and we'll never know why she chose Jerry to tear apart and why the others were free of verbal diarrhea. Maybe because he was the youngest and left her to pursue his dreams and explore. Maybe because he evolved, and she didn't. It sounds familiar.

I suppose it was my own pain and alone time with God that allowed me to be accountable and recognize I missed Jerry's signs, not because I regret our life together, but because I believed he had the perfect upbringing, later learning there may be no such thing.

How could he love me with the love, praise and affection he did not receive? How could he offer me unpained love when his mother did not nurture, treasure or give him unconditional love the way loving mothers are supposed to give?

I've read that we draw what we know. My head doctor will say, "You married Gloria." I suppose I did in some ways, but knowing and acknowledging is power, and I have the power to make it better because I choose better. The choice has always been mine.

Marriage is hard, particularly when a spicy Latina and a fiery Italian are forced to grow up together, to challenge each other's shortcomings and strengths. I knew marriage would be challenging, raw and honest, but I also knew it would be fun, lovely and revealing.

At the end of the day, even though we all want to connect, love, belong and create, it is up to us to make a decision to change the mother signature when the signature needs tweaks and upgrades. It is up to us and only us to learn and use the bad for good, to be eternally and obnoxiously hopeful, curious and optimistic for a bigger and brighter future. It's always up to us because we are all individually worthy of love, and we always have a choice in the matter.

27

A CHILD IS MADE

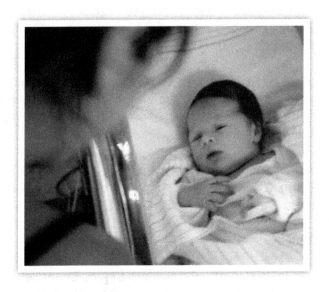

Kyra was made with love during the autumn of 2000 in a garage that Bob, Jerry's second brother, converted into a habitable space just outside of Seattle.

Jerry and I had flown there for Bob and Janice's wedding. Bob was the one they thought would never marry, the quietest of the four brothers.

To prepare for the wedding and the inbound Pacific clan arriving from New Jersey, Florida and California, Bob the builder who makes a practice of building his homes with his own two hands, managed to convert his garage into the comfortable and cozy space for Jerry and me to occupy, away from the wedding madness taking place in the main house.

The scene was country like, laid out over five acres of land, long roads and quiet cricket symphony. Cool autumn adorned the ground and trees with beautiful amber, orange and burgundy leaves, and once inside the new converted space with pretty gleaming lights throughout, it was the perfect scene for baby making when we forgot to practice the ancient rhythm method that would give us a child.

After the wedding, in Los Angeles, I vividly felt something was off. I didn't know what exactly, but as a woman who knows her body well, I knew something was different. After a few days of these unsettling feelings, I realized I might be pregnant, confirmed when my OB/GYN said so.

This is what I knew immediately:
I knew she was a girl.
I knew she would be fantastic.
I knew she would be healthy.
I knew I was going to like her a lot.
I knew she'd teach me treasures.
I knew I would be in awe of her every day.
I knew she would challenge me.
I knew she would challenge me a lot.
I knew I had to get out of my way
    and raise her according to her needs and not my lack of.
I knew she'd be tall.
I knew she'd be fun.
I knew it'd be an honor to be her mom.
I knew I would love being pregnant, and I did,
    I LOVED every second.
I knew she would be smart and would probably outsmart me.
I knew she'd challenge Jerry immensely.
I knew I had to help him.
I knew he'd make many mistakes.
I knew I'd probably make more.
I knew I'd have to let her make mistakes.
I knew I'd have to let her spread her wings.

I knew I wanted to help her learn to fly.
I knew I'd have to catch her when she fell.
I knew I'd have to let her fly on her own.
I knew I'd mess up at mothering her.
I knew I'd try my best at the job.
I knew I'd do anything for her.
I knew I loved her already, in the womb.

Being pregnant with her was a blast. I felt sexier than I feel now. I felt empowered, strong, alive, happy and womanly. It was an honor to carry her.

And while I loved carrying my little peanut and experiencing the magic of nurturing her from the womb, I had one very important concern I needed to discuss with the doctor.

"Doc, you need to know something very important."

"Yes, what is it?" he responded with a mild smirk.

"I will probably not be able push when you ask. I have absolutely no pain tolerance," I shared with great conviction.

"You'll be fine. Don't get ahead of yourself." He smiled, but I was certain he'd never met a chicken like me.

"I don't think you understand, Doc, I have zero pain tolerance, like ZERO. Please know that going in, mainly because I do not want to stress my baby during delivery." He acknowledged my concern, which led me to believe I was heard and the pain department would be taken care by his many years of pulling babies out crotches.

I walked away convinced he would take care of any pain in the delivery because I believed in fairies.

Once I began to get bigger and hungrier, prettier and

ravenous, a small issue began to surface, one that bothered me greatly. The exit way was not flowing as usual, the only unpleasant part of pregnancy, and the bigger I became the worse it was.

I have always been a fan of the body disposing of what it no longer needs. It could be the Virgo in me. Even so, it is the natural flow of the human anatomy, and being plugged up while carrying a child was a preoccupation that needed a solution quickly.

I mainly thought about my baby's nutrition. I wanted to make sure things were digesting and flushing out as they should so that she was properly nourished.

After speaking with the doctor, who already thought I was nuts, someone mentioned a simple solution that has been around for gazillion years... fiber. It must have been my pregnant brain because I should have known. I had worked in a health food store, and fiber is health 101.

After much research and shopping, fibrous protein-filled pancakes, salads, vegetables, endless meatballs that Kyra demanded from the womb and walks twice a day on the Strand, my body began to work better than before being pregnant. However, it was the meatballs I craved and ate like they were going out of style. It could have been the iron or tomato. Whatever it was, Kyra sent a daily craving for tasty, moist meatballs.

Our bodies are machines that need our assistance to work properly. It is our job to treat them better than we treat our cars, or things will go haywire. I took this sentiment seriously when pregnant, so much so that I began to lose weight while following my fibrous, healthy and active routine.

"Thirty pounds, Karina. You need to gain at least 30 pounds,"

Doc pleaded.

"Don't worry about it, Doc. You're getting ahead of yourself. And I don't like silly generic rules. I'm eating well and walking. You should be proud of me." He smiled without disagreeing.

Time was ticking, 39 weeks and no contractions, no dilation or signs of Kyra wanting to meet us, and frankly, I didn't mind. I didn't want her out yet.

"No rush, you stay there as long as you need," I told her while rubbing my enormous, perfectly formed belly. I knew this time was fleeting. The time she and I were one. I knew that, after bearing her, my job would change to nurturing her and equipping her to fly with her own wings in this wild and smoggy city I love.

However, Kyra was now running out of embryotic fluid and needed to be induced by 41 weeks tops, if not before.

On the day scheduled to make magic happen with the help of the fairies in my head who'd keep me from any physical pain, Pitocin and an epidural made their way through my bloodstream with no luck. Kyra had no intention in vacating my insides. She was warm, cozy and probably drugged up at this point. We waited for hours leaving the doctor with only one solution, to pull her out of my crotch with a vacuum suction plunger-like apparatus. It seemed barbaric...who would have thought this would be my fairy delivery and Kyra's first entrance to the world?

As if vacuuming her was not enough as she slept through the entire beastly suction process, I tore all the way to the back as the doctor pulled her out of my being. "This is what they call a vaginal tear," he said, composed while trying to figure the mess between my legs. I looked at him with foggy confusion.

No one prepared us for this, not that I attended Lamaze classes.

It all happened too fast. Fear and joy were mixed up in one, and after our sleepy cone-head baby was pulled out, I looked to Jerry.

"She's not crying. Tell him to spank her." I began to tear up.

The doctor spanked her lightly, and this would be her first introduction into the world, a spank on her little hiney. He talked to her; he cleaned her up, but nothing. She was quiet, chill and slightly blue.

These are the moments when fear elevates itself to the highest level. These are the moments when nothing else in the world matters. These are the moments when one's own heart stops.

Jerry was frozen until he did what he did best when Kyra was in the womb. He sang to her.

During my last trimester, when Kyra began her nightly ritual of kicking, flipping and passing her fingers through my tummy until late hours, Jerry made a habit of singing to her by placing his face against my belly vibrating the deep lyrics of "Ol' Man River" against my moving human ball, skin to skin.

He picked the song for the depth in the voice as in the original, while connecting with her via vibration and tone calming Kyra every time. Jerry singing "Ol' Man River" was the act that offered us the most beautiful cry as the depth of his voice danced into her new eardrums, a monumental relief in a time of uncertainty.

Jerry's singing also helped by distracting me from pure fearful agony, while puzzling the nurses, some of whom were black.

The doctor had no idea what was going on. His job was to deliver a healthy baby.

The moment a baby cries, things move faster than the eye can follow. My vaginal tear was being stitched up without my knowing, after the placenta made its way out, quickly followed by nurses undressing and dressing the doctor with new scrubs after all the mess I had discharged on him, also without my knowing.

Kyra was being cleaned and handed back and forth from nurse to nurse, and machines were being monitored all while Oprah observed the entire bloody mess from the top corner of the room.

And then that moment happened. That moment in a mother's life when nothing else matters but the little being that has been made. The first moment she and I met eye to eye, the moment I fell deeply in love with the most beautiful individual I had ever met. But just like that, things keep moving. Our moment was short lived to now transform myself into a milk-producing machine.

It is ridiculous how fast it all goes. That was my moment with her, and now that my insides were done carrying her, I needed to offer another part of my body to continue the nourishing process.

The female body is one fascinating and badass machine. There is no other way to appreciate the enormity of what it can do, all of which I appreciate with every cell of my being.

After a day of squeezing my nipples with machine-like movements and manipulations while massaging my breasts to begin the process to produce breast milk, Kyra like the magical being that she is, latched on like a pro, a bizarre moment, and amazing beyond comprehension.

She and I became one again for those moments of nourishment. How did she learn that? I wondered while staying present in her moment of need. But I could not stop my mind from what had just happened. She had just been in the womb attached to me by an umbilical cord; it's not like she had pre-delivery training in there. She simply moved her mouth all around the breast until she found the nipple and drank away after a little help pulling down her bottom lip for a better latch. It was human connection at its rawest.

These natural stages in life, although sounding simple, still astonish me with speechless appreciation for the human species, for the mother and daughter connection, one I honor greatly.

We finally settled in with our baby Kyra on the first day in the hospital as everyone announced all was good and it was time to rest. Then Jerry pronounced, "I stink like hospital. I shall return." He kissed Kyra and me on the forehead and headed home to update the family and shower.

The nurse brought Kyra back to my bed so we could rest, and I tried to breastfeed her again while observing the little being I had just made in my insides. I looked at her browless face realizing life was all about her now, and I was excited to follow her journey.

As we snuggled and bonded, all was well until I heard a slight something; something was off with her. I didn't know what, but I knew my gut feeling needed attention.

I placed her closer to me to feel her rhythm, the space she now occupied, and that's when I realized her breathing was off. Jerry was gone and I panicked, quickly beeping the nurse over and over until one ran into my room.

"She's not breathing well. It feels like she's skipping," I told the nurse as she whisked her away from me.

I did consider my state of mind being that I was detoxing from bags of Petocin, two epidurals and Vicodins to aid my vaginal tear, quickly acknowledging it was not in my head. Kyra needed help.

I sat in that room alone, sobbing having just handed my baby over with no comfort in sight. I got cold and small in the world until the doctor returned to inform me that Kyra was on her way to NICU. His words were a blur as I looked deep into his eyes trying to see fear or hope. He was mumbling as far as I was concerned only remembering:

"Your baby has a little pocket in her breathing pathway that needs catching up. With a little antibiotic and some rest, she'll be fine, but she will have to be in ICU until she finishes her antibiotic and for observation."

"I don't understand. I need to call my husband. He was dirty," I said barely making up words.

"Where is your husband?"

"In the shower."

"In the hospital?"

"No, our house, he was dirty. I need to call him. I don't understand," I responded while losing myself in tears, cold and alone.

There was joy, pain and excitement for a new life and connection, now there was fear and uncertainty.

28

RAISING MAGIC

Steve Jobs said, "Live each day as if it was your last." The thought is obvious, leaning on cliché, particularly when we make daily choices to get wrapped up in nonsense, quickly forgetting the bottom line: this day may very well be your last.

Lives can shift in one teeny-tiny second. Life can change without our knowing making us forget what we've had for breakfast because we have failed to enjoy every bite and savor it like it was the last bite.

So I remind you, "Live each day as if it was your last" because it would be rare to duplicate the day, and we don't know when it will be our last on Earth and with those we love.

That moment, when I was cold and alone in the hospital room wondering what would become of my barely day-old child, it felt as it could be my last. I quickly understood the unspoken love of a mother for her offspring, even if the meet and greet was short.

I pleaded to the nurse to contact Jerry, to ask him to return. It would be several days later that seemed like years when I felt it was all going to be ok. In hindsight, Kyra's condition was a mild and short NICU emergency case, but at that moment, our lives stopped as human beings. Nothing else mattered.

Kyra resided in the hospital six nights, seven days, four more after I was discharged. We stayed in the hospital every moment we could, especially since Kyra had grown quite fond of the boob and clearly needed to be fed.

Nurses offered to feed her in the middle of the night so I could rest. Feeding entailed pumped milk through a bottle, but I could not fathom another woman holding her to do the job that was mine. "It will confuse Kyra," I thought. Kyra was too new to the world to have to understand. The choice was a soft nipple with warm milk on demand or a strangely shaped bottle nipple dispensing overheated recently refrigerated leche. I was doing the thinking for Kyra. It was not a tough call.

Although still terrified beyond comprehension, I knew Kyra would be ok because I knew she had God, just like me. I have that much faith. He had always been on my side, and the same would make sense for Kyra who came from me. However, the uncertainty lay in the medical briefs from staff that unsettled me. NICU staff, as amazing as they are, have jobs to do, to monitor the patient in need, not the zombie parents with the nerves of crazy person. And every NICU parent has the nerves of a crazy person.

The NICU will humble anyone with a heartbeat. There were many infants and premies during Kyra's stay. The sounds of the machines were unnerving, and rows of tiny infants with tubes and lights can break anybody's heart. Every day we visited the NICU, we passed a little boy with a strong case of jaundice who cried endlessly while lying under the light to balance his coloring. He cried with a sad somberness and a distinct rhythm and despair making me believe he was aware of his initial place in the world and was saddened by it. He cried and cried while I had to keep myself from picking him up to console and hug him. The only thing that stopped me was the possibility of getting sued, because unfortunately, we live in a sue-happy existence. So I leaned down, face to face, hoping he felt company in the presence I offered.

NICU days reminded me of the times I accompanied Lucia during her leukemia treatments at Children's Hospital. They reminded me of the most important wealth in our lives, our health.

Kyra's last day in the NICU could not come too soon. I clearly remember heading home realizing how consumed I had been the last seven days. I had forgotten how beautiful blue skies were, what fresh air smelled like, what it felt like to take a long, calm shower and the simplicity of drinking delicious water. Life had stopped without my noticing. Kyra was free and clear, and I was ready to receive any goodness God had planned for us.

Raising a daughter, raising Kyra, has been one of the best, most challenging, eye-opening, teaching, growing, humbling, angering, funny, compassionate, revealing, loving and surrendering thing I've ever done. I've loved every moment, even the tough ones.

Challenging moments were those fearful times when doubt crept up and occupied my mind praying that she was not being groomed by a sick man or woman who aimed to steal the innocence we'd nurtured. Having been sexually abused by both genders, I knew their game, the crafting, manipulation, the deceit in their caring and the time freely invested by the predator. I know how good they are and how the game can be played. I know that when they have a target, they have studied it and followed it. They are meticulously patient to ultimately satisfy their perversion for as long as they can get away with it while maintaining great intimacy, secrecy and shame. And once they have acquired their victim's secrecy and shame, it's playtime for the sick. My job was to keep this from her life while not infusing my own fear into her childhood.

After the customary six-week maternity leave, I went back to work full-time at the local spa as an esthetician, waxer and skincare manager, which meant forty-plus hours a week. And because Jerry and I could not fathom having a stranger care for our infant, Gloria would be our savior and reveal herself as a better grandmother to Kyra than a mother to me. The only issue would be the boob, my boobs, and that Jerry and I would have to work it out somehow.

Jerry worked nights at a local private club while auditioning during the day and taking care of Kyra when Gloria could not.

We should have bought stock in the amount of bottles, fake nipples and contraptions we invested in Babies R Us. Unfortunately for Jerry who yearned to bottle feed her, Kyra would have none of it. She wanted what she wanted, and she wanted the boob for nourishment, not a plastic pretend nipple that was probably designed and manufactured by a man who had mommy issues. They were all too hard for her.

This made Jerry go Jersey with a dash of Italian when he'd throw every bottle through the house frustrated when every plastic nipple we bought in every store was rejected with Kyra's lips closing shut. Jerry's efforts lasted longer than an infant's patience. She wailed until she got the boob, and once she caught her breath and latched on, a bottle thrown across the room would head one way and a grown man stomping the other, frustrated that he could not feed his child and bond with her like I did. The effort was heartfelt; the frustration cost us hundreds of dollars; and the helpless dad was called "The Bear" as a result.

While he threw a legitimate tantrum, I brainstormed to figure out how I could feed Kyra every three hours in the middle of my work shifts, in between back-to-back facials and waxing vaginas. The struggle was real, but feeding our child was the priority, even if there were infant and grown-man tantrums along the way.

By the grace of will and desire to care for our boobie lover who needed freshly squeezed warm milk every three hours on the dot, Jerry and I made it work, no excuses. No sacrifice was too big. We signed up for the job, but it didn't feel like a job; it was unconditional.

Around this time, Jerry and I had begun our struggles as a newly married couple as a result of our complex mothers and our own issues. A sassy Latina and an Italian from South Jersey are bound to challenge one another from time to time with the strong character and passion our cultures offer. But where Kyra was concerned, Jerry and I were always in sync from the day she was conceived.

And without much discussion, we made it work. During my workdays every 2.45 hours, Jerry drove two miles from our house to the spa. He dashed in with our hungry child and handed her to me in a little room of the spa in enough time to relieve Kyra's hungry belly with my engorged milk-producing tetas, five minutes on each side. I kissed her and quickly handed her back to Jerry, "the burping master" that he became with enough time for me to change the sheets in my skincare room for another facial or waxing client ready for a "south of the border" landscaping service for her weekend getaway. This was our reality for thirteen months until Kyra decided she had enough of the boob and went on to a sippy cup, leaving me with painfully engorged boobs I had to wean from production. And that was that. With one simple action and decision, Kyra told me her milk needs were no longer needed.

A few weeks after that, she continued her journey of independence when she learned how to walk with arms up for balance and Boo Monsters Inc. pigtails for cuteness. That's when Kyra got really fun as she began to make words to communicate with us and an insatiable laughter only Jerry can elicit.

The more she developed, the more it became clear Kyra needed more than Gloria could offer even though they had developed a special grandmother-granddaughter bond in their own way.

I imagined this would have been the stage in my life where Gloria would have shone with care and nurturing but didn't because she was working.

As for Gloria, she understood in her own non-communicative way Kyra's craving for social interaction as she began to attend a couple of days of daycare where she learned art and crafts, which did not come easy for Gloria and me.

Kyra's fluid reach to make new friendships from the start was effortless and admirable. It disarmed the grumpiest of kids, making our days at the park revealing of her personality to come and a great place to see her discover her world, while I was being chased by the local nannies.

"How much do you get paid?" a woman asked.

"For what?" I responded

"Oh, are you a live-in nanny? Do you cook for the family?"

"Are you kidding me? I don't get paid. I do this for free; I'm her mother, Señora."

I'd laugh and walk away realizing there was a nanny gossip world I had not been aware of, some of whom were my own people. I don't know if I was taken aback for not having been recognized as one of their own or insulted for the gossip attached to money.

One of the most valuable unspoken lessons Gloria gave me was her work ethic, and although she struggled as a single mom doing the job for two offering the best she could, a humble life compared to those around us, money was never discussed positively or negatively, and I never felt a lack because of it. Money was a private matter and not to be gossiped about or shared unless there was business to be discussed.

Working weekends at the spa meant I missed kids' weekend parties, and after many of them Jerry would have to attend as a weekend caretaking dad. It was one of many where he'd meet a friend for life himself.

"Jerry, Kyra has a party for a kid in her daycare class. His name is Gabriel."

"How does Kyra get invited to daycare birthday parties? It's not like Gabriel asked her. They're in daycare, for God's sake. They can barely speak a full sentence." Jerry has always been able to combine humor with common sense.

"Do we know any adults at the party? I never know anyone, and I'm usually the only sucker at those things," Jerry said.

"I don't think so. You'll love this party, though. It's in the Santa Monica Pier. You will love the Carousel room where the party is," I responded trying to pump him up.

"Am I being bamboozled here, Santa Monica?"

"You never know what life brings, Jerry!" And I walked away before he had a chance to say another word.

I have always been in awe of kids' birthday parties in Los Angeles. Here, kids get face painting and dance parties, photo booths, rented venues and even closing down a block to make a three-year-old feel special. Back home, it was a cake, balloons, grouchy family faces and one picture for proof.

So Jerry, the curmudgeon, headed to Santa Monica Pier with his three-year-old pigtailed beauty, not knowing a single soul in the party. Later he realized it was a good day for him as well, when he gained a friend for life meeting the father of the birthday boy. "Great things happen when bamboozled," I said to the "The Bear." Mike and Milly, now near and forever dear friends.

Mike and Jerry created a sweet friendship sharing fatherhood, food, wine, cigars and style, wardrobe style that is.

During my time being "single with God," male friendships became a norm, a norm I used to observe and learn the male psyche. I wanted to know what would make a man abandon his daughter, why a male becomes a pedophile, and why numbnuts are created. I wanted to understand the opposite sex a little deeper in an effort to avoid another knucklehead, and possibly marry one. While I garnered male friendships along the way who continue to help me understand how a husband and father thinks, I never encountered metrosexuals like Jerry and Mike who share a love for shopping, apparel, designers and fits. I do have to say, their shopping outings for the wives before the holidays are kind of cute, while they throw in a piece or two for themselves.

Once in kindergarten at the nearby Catholic school, Kyra locked eyes with Georgia. It was friendship at first sight. They sealed a friendship and so would the dads, whose mutual friendship and respect have shown the girls what life is all about.

The older I get, only shown by the fine lines along my eyes from some pain and lots of laughter elicited by Jerry and gray hair I now pay to cover, I wonder what I could have done better. What if I missed an opportunity to teach her something of deeper substance, wiser words and actions? What if... what if? I find myself grieving teaching opportunities that seemed too obvious the day after, but I failed the opportunity because I was too preoccupied with life. What if?

And while I try to avoid the "what if" torture, I remind myself of some of the things I have gotten right, some of the basics, like when she lost it for no reason and all she needed was a hug. Or those magic moments when she shared stories about friendships and school and I listened because that's all she needed. Or those sweet moments I caught her watching me apply makeup, only to realize she's doing almost the same on her own perfectly shaped face. It's these simple moments of connection that overwrite most "what ifs." Until the hormones emerged.

I don't know where I pulled it all from. I choose to think it was all God because I sure as hell was not equipped the way a teen should have been.

"Kyra, as you may know, a woman's body is amazing. It is

also very complex and always evolving. Your hormones will be coming in soon. You are a tween. Your emotions will shift from happy to sad or pissed off. You are a beautiful mix of Mexican, Spanish, Italian, Irish and German, so when you get pissed off, it could be all of that or your hormones. Either way, I love you and won't be able to help unless you tell me how."

She was quiet. It seemed like her tween self was listening. I don't know if she was trying work it all in her sweet complex stage of life, or if she thought I was crazy, but she never stopped me.

"What are hormones?" Kyra asked.

"Well, your body is getting ready. Your hormones are working themselves into your system as you get ready to enter puberty, your period. And when a gal gets her period, typically in her teen years, it's a VERY exciting time. We should celebrate you on your way to being a young lady."

And gauging her attentiveness, I'd continue.

"But before that, before your period, hormones will kick in, making you emotional, short tempered or moody. You may crave certain foods and feel constipated somewhere in the process, but if you pay attention to your body and get to know its rhythm, it won't be so bad. Getting to know your body is not only empowering, but necessary. Kyra, I'm here to help you, but I encourage you to try to get to know your body's patterns so it does not take you over."

The conversations varied, and the words spilled based on learning it all by myself. She always listened.

Over the years, we talked about healthy and toxic friendships (maybe mirroring my life, speaking out loud hoping to get rid of the toxic ones I was clinging to). We spoke of butterfly crushes, in hopes she'd share her first one with me. We spoke of the memorable first kiss, "Choose well and make it a good one. You'll always remember that one, just like the first time you have sex." Yes, I snuck in the S E X word not forgetting to mention first, second and third base, which could lead to danger, desires you may not be ready for. Oh yeah, somehow, I managed to sneak in conversations about drugs, emotional shopping, bargains, skincare, makeup, tampons and so on. When I keep it short and sweet, she rarely stops me.

I suppose my oversharing leaned on a slight case of self-therapy. It would have been nice if Gloria had had in her to cover some basics when I was growing up, like the monthlies and how to use a tampon, well, that was embarrassing.

It was pathetic and in my older years during a friend's birthday pool party at the Beverly Hills Hotel when my life changed with a simple little plug.

When I couldn't swim due to my monthly, my sweet and very modest friend, Kerry, could not fathom me going through life this way.

"Why aren't you coming in the pool?" Kerry asked.

"I'm on my period."

"WHAT? C'mon. Are you telling me you've never used a tampon?"

Kerry's character has always been measured, low key, modest and intelligent, but my tampon situation bounced her out of the pool in no time leading us on a wild goose chase throughout the beautiful palm tree hotel to teach me a very private matter. After asking the bellboy and several cleaning gals, Kerry and I found ourselves in the restroom, next to the Polo Lounge with a door separating one another.

Kerry instructed: "Bend your legs, BUT not too much." After a few trial and errors, and thankfully no one entering the restroom during the teaching session, she forever changed my life. Needless to say, I'd be the one to teach Kyra all the tampon business.

As for Gloria, she was never equipped for those conversations, for any of them. She tried, though.

"Kari, why are your breasts so big?" she'd ask with a deep frown bordering on judgment.

"Why do you think?"

"Ahi, Karina, why are you the way you are?" as she walked away.

She tried, possibly scaring herself with her efforts.

Time flies so darn fast. Why is Kyra a teenager so quickly? Where did our baby Kyra go? How was I breastfeeding yesterday and now we're visiting colleges? Have I covered enough material? Please, God, equip me with the answers she requires.

And while I do this mothering thing without having been mothered, from a blank slate I choose to believe the *lack of* has been my greatest strength. And by the grace of God, I'm able to use the past for teaching and strength while omitting the "what if's" and doubts.

I signed up for this. I always knew I wanted to be a mother, and I knew I was going to be a good one. I just didn't know I was going to question myself so much. Maneuvering humble beginnings in Mexico and the streets of East LA might have been easier, but I wouldn't change a thing. Raising magic, raising Kyra, has been an honor.

29

THIS THING CALLED MARRIAGE -YES DEAR!

I suppose I wanted a marriage. It seemed to be something to strive for, a common goal I heard people talk about, like when they say, I want to lose weight, but the struggle is not losing weight, it's keeping if off. A necessary evil.

"I can't wait to fall in love."
"I can't wait to meet a guy."
"I want to be married," girlfriends said.

I, on the other hand, wondered:
"Why the rush?"
"It's such a big gamble. Why the fairytale need?"

"What is this marriage thing everyone talks about and seems to want, yet so many fail?"

I imagine I wanted to avoid being part the 40 percent of divorcees in America, what seems to be now a norm. On the flip side, I knew I'd fail only if I failed to try, and that, I didn't like at all.

I had been too busy catching up with life to give marriage the appropriate thought and attention it deserves. It seemed like a thing I needed to do, particularly after having been asked for my hand in marriage three times. The question became a numb relationship routine.

A lack of happy partnerships and marriages will make anyone cautious too, why I became a "runaway bride." Poor marriage examples in my youth, lack of a father, or Gloria's lack of explanation may have been the reason I unknowingly colluded with numbnuts in my life, reiterating that marriage is not all that's cracked up to be. It's one vicious cycle. "I will marry you" is not the same as an "I do." Nothing was signed, and that's as far as I'll go. I'm ok with that.

And because I had not given marriage the appropriate thought and attention it rightfully deserves, shaking off unresolved childhood issues while married can certainly put a damper on the first decade of any marriage. Sex ran the course of our tantrums and our ups and downs, while we lacked the most important ingredient a marriage can own, intimacy.

Ironically, the exchange of familiar childhood notes and the heartaches that come with it made for a closer bond, closer *intimacy* that I didn't think was a thing, because why would I know? Intimacy, a silent bond a couple builds when they surrender to each other, a bond that needs nurturing and cannot be bought.

After sixteen years of riding the rollercoaster of marriage, learning to fully enjoy the highs while hanging on tight for the lows, I suppose I've learned to like this thing called marriage. It's been worth the ride.

Marriage is hard. There's no way around it, yet it's a blast. Marriage reveals the best and worst of us. It forces us to dig deep if we're awake enough for the effort because without the conscientious effort, one may end up in the 40 percent.

Marriage forces us to:
Grow up
Compromise
Share
Consider
Rise with
Fall with
Ache for
Cheer for
Consult with
Challenge
Surrender to
Say, "Yes, dear"

I changed it. I really did. I changed the cycle. I went for it and broke my mold. I changed my story. It took work. It took effort. It brought me tears, helpless on my knees, tears of pain and laughter. We, after all, may end up happily ever after.

Jerry and I continue to raise our magical Kyra, our teen who has run the course with us enduring growth, conflict, resolution and much welcomed laughter that Jerry elicits from the smallest of things. I think we've done all right.

I'll keep on leaning on God for His loving and everlasting guidance and support, while staying awake, open and having a blast in the journey.

"Jerry, if it wasn't for the faith we have in common, your good looks and daily comedy, I would have dropped you like a bad habit long ago."

"Bite me," says The Bear.

30

MY HERE AND MY NOW

My here and my now is simple because I've designed it that way.

My here and my now is to be here, present and in the now as often as I can with the people I choose to be with, accompanied by humor, laughter and my best along the way.

My here and my now is to continue to follow my motto, that life is good, that life is as magical, simple and complicated as I make it and that drama or worldly distractions are to be avoided like the plague.

As I look back at my life, my story, I'm thankful to be able to learn from the past with great clarity and obnoxious magical positivity, even if it annoys some.

I choose to think the clarity I've gained is a mix bag of the good and the bad in my childhood, from work and personal ups and downs and being a mother, which certainly puts things in perspective when the perspective is allowed.

My here and my now is blessings and work in progress. It is the small and big milestones I've created for myself from nothing, from dirt roads, cold showers, fruitful humble beg innings and naïve eagerness that have given me big and small wins to cheer for and carry me on.

Big and small wins celebrated with my own dance and song memorable enough to remind me to do it again, to keep dancing, to keep moving on, to stand tall.

Life is not easy at times. Being a good daughter can be challenging. Being an honest friend can be hard. Parenting the future is a big responsibility. Marriage can certainly be a mind fuck from time to time and working in the service industry all my life certainly taught me things not learned in school. With it all, life is good because it is. It's that simple. And because there are human beings somewhere in the world who'd pray for the things I call struggles. But there's always the missing tile.

After many years searching for my missing tile and healing my open father wound by means of private investigators and the internet, a healer, would put my heart to rest.

I wondered if he'd come through from the other side, which would mean he had died, and if he did, I'd have an answer and end the search. But he didn't come through. It was, however, Jerry's late father, my father in law Fred, sweet, wonderful Fred, who came through in a session confirming himself through Debra, the healer.

She laughed slightly with love in her face, the same love that exuded from Fred. Maybe I wanted to see it; it felt genuine. She described his posture, demeanor, clothes and laughter with words I understood. It was Fred.

"I've got my eye on you. You will be ok," he said.

And that was enough, all I needed. The search for my father was peacefully over and done. It became ok to rest and let go. I realized I not only have God looking after me, but I have Fred, who exemplified the love of a great father and the kind who loved his kids and family greatly.

Although it would have been nice to have had a Fred during my entire life, God sent me angels on earth, positive male figures along my journey, like my uncle, who I walked and conversed with about the beautiful Mexican culture running through our veins; my cousin Beto, who gave me the gift of exercise, movement and outdoors; Mr. Kinder, who gave me music and more than he'll ever know; Shan, who said very little but, when he did, it was gold; and sweet Fred, his loving soul was icing on the cake.

I have been blessed. It was time to let it go and be.

Life moves so quickly, and we never know what tomorrow holds. So I'll keep choosing to look for the good in all, to view life with childlike magic, with much laughter, forgiveness for trespasses onto me and me to others, while staying true to self because I'm onto something. My gut tells me so.

"The most liberating thing about beauty is realizing that you are the beholder," actress Salma Hayek noted. Warren Buffett believes in "Kiss": Keep It Simple, Stupid, to which I add, "You have the power to lean into the positive or negative. Chose well and add some fun." That sums it up for me.

My here and my now is a continued, overzealously gracious heart for God's grace and love because without Him, I just don't know.

31

SHE CHOSE

This is a story about a girl who, against some odds, challenges and setbacks, chose the possibility in all she saw. She chose magic, even in the darkest of times.

She was born with a light that illuminated her journey's gloom and a burning fire that urged her to rise above deep-seated roots.

This is a story of a girl whose curiosity paved her way, with a quest to find her story. She walked through borders and routes in search of truth, her truth, finding doses of humanity, lessons and beauty along her way.

This is a story about a girl who holds eternal hope and

optimism, while others tell her "hold on, I don't work that way." She doesn't stall; a light keeps her moving.

She's not famous, not rich and doesn't own an expensive car. She is imperfectly perfect being a mother, a daughter, a wife and friend. Her life is simple. She loves her journey and gleams her future. She chose.

She chose good. She chose love. She chose bigger. She chose God. Above all, she chose to change what she was given. She chose.

32

STUFF I'VE LEARNED

You have the power to lean into positive or negative. Choose well and add some fun.

We have the power to choose either one in the way we are, talk, act and give. We always have a choice, whether we see it or not. The choice is there.

Remind yourself to lean into the possibility in everything and add some fun. Choose kindness, choose goodness, choose love, even if it wasn't given to you. It's your choice to choose and have fun in the process.

Wake up with gratitude every day.

Gratitude for the big and small things has literally saved my life.

I don't usually wake up happy or gracious. I usually want ten more minutes. But when I'm finally awake, after a cup of coffee, I am quickly overtaken with gratefulness for every basic and grand thing in my life. From the immense amount of humanity people have shown me along the way to the hard lessons I chose to learn from.

Find your way to dig deep and make a practice to be grateful. Show graciousness for the beauty in every day because every day, if you look hard enough, there is something to be grateful for.

Make it a habit, make it a good one.

Victim no more.

Shit happens to everyone. There is not one perfect individual with the perfect life.

Erasing victimhood from my mindset and vocabulary has empowered me more than I can describe. Hand in hand with gratitude, my victimless mindset has also saved my life leaving me room for greatness. It beats walking through life feeling sorry for myself and blaming people for things.

When I feel I have been wronged, I take long, reflective walks while learning from the trespass, ultimately empowering myself. It's not always easy, but it's the best option under any circumstance.

Giving victimhood power is like giving one's self away for free.

Be nice to all. Everyone is important.

When Gloria worked, I was pawned off from house to house, place to place offering me one of the best lessons in life. Whether I was being dropped off with dirt-poor family or the unnecessarily rich, the vast array of people along the way with different social status taught me that, at the end of the day, we're all human beings. And we are all equally important maneuvering almost the same issues and needs. Everyone has more and less of things that are ultimately "things." What remains is being a human being.

Be good to everyone. To the homeless person down the street, the enemy or the one adorned with jewels and wealth. Everyone is important with a different, yet alike, set of issues.

Everyone has a story. Find the good in yours and add to it.

Throughout my life, I found that everyone has their unique own story and that no one's story is perfect. Asking questions and listening to people's lives, and what they take away, has helped me understand people, life and myself. We have the power to teach each other seamlessly.

Learn from everyone's life and their magic while adding goodness to yours.

Let's agree to disagree.

I have found that during complex and opposing topics, "agreeing to disagree" benefits everyone involved, particularly the topic at hand. Learning and understanding the opposite side benefits everyone involved while amicably exchanging opposing opinions. Otherwise, the discussion ends, and that is boring.

Forgive and grieve.

We're human beings, which means we're imperfect. Someone or something is bound to wrong us from time to time until the end of our days.

Find ways to make peace with it or them while finding the lesson in it. When the lesson is revealed and learned, forgiveness typically follows. If it's not enough, grieve it and send it off. The rest is not for you to carry. Like Elsa said in the movie Frozen, "Let it go."

Holding a grudge holds greatness and freedom.

Be curious and stay curious.

Back home, while Gloria worked and was too busy to teach me about life, being curious was my pastime.

I watched everything and everyone who took care of me with great insight. And when I didn't understand why people did the things they did, they later showed me with their actions and words.

Be curious about everything and everyone, and be amazed at the big and small things life places in front of you every day. They are there for a reason.

Learn to let your mind explore newness, even if it's uncomfortable. I'm a firm believer that having an open mind and being curious about everything in life is key to living fully and to longevity.

Be curious, keep learning and don't stop.

You don't know it all. Ask questions.

When you don't know something, say you don't and ask. You're not going to melt if you do. It's ok to ask questions and not know everything.

I made peace with this long ago when I was too shy to ask, and I felt I should know. It's ok not to know, and I'm only short- changing myself by trying to pretend I do.

The only dumb question is the one not asked.

Say you're sorry and let the burden set you free.

This one is hard for many, including myself.

Say you're sorry when sorry is due. Saying sorry doesn't make anyone less than if the sorry is warranted. Learn to feel the freedom in the word. It's better for everyone involved, particularly yourself.

Hug, hug big or not at all.

I remember the first real hug I received from a stranger like it was yesterday. It was the kindest, most genuine embrace anyone had ever given me. It was healing and profound.

This simple gesture can offer a large impact on any human being, even the least affectionate stiff.

I also remember the worst hug I've received. That's all I have to say about that.

So let it go. Open your arms and hug, hug often and hug big, particularly your loved ones.

Learn to read people.

I suppose I learned this as a way of survival in Mexico and while working in the service industry all of my life.

It takes practice and observation, but learning to read people is not only fascinating, it is also an amazing tool for life and work. I love to observe quirks, responses, gestures, habits and patterns while learning from them. We all have them.

We are all uniquely fascinating and each other's teachers.

Compliment things and people.

Gloria never complimented me, but she also never criticized me. Having no baseline on this topic gave me the opportunity to choose my own way. I chose to be positive and to compliment.

Sharing genuine and honest compliments with my family, friends, strangers, even Rosie, my dog, is very healing and empowering to all parties involved.

Everyone has a great quality and has beauty of some kind.

Find it and compliment away. It makes everyone feel good, you in particular.

Constructive criticism with love.

There's nothing worse than a professional critic. I find it better to give constructive criticism, as opposed to simply criticize.

When offering kind constructive criticism, both parties participate. Both parties grow. Criticizing alone is lazy, and it says more about your shortcomings than the person you're criticizing.

When giving constructive criticism, do it with love.

There are many sides to any story.

During conflict, there are typically many sides to a story. There is everyone's story based on what they individually took from it, based on their emotions, and then there is the God's honest truth that He sees from above.

When your opinion is needed, try to stay open minded and keep in mind that the truth lies somewhere in between everyone's version of their side of the story.

Thank all.

When receiving, always say "thank you."

This simple gesture is so easy to forget that I forget. Thank everyone and everything. Say it out loud.

Be your own cheerleader and pat yourself on the back.

Having little encouragement or support when growing up meant I had to rely on myself for inspiration of any kind, especially during lonesome times when I couldn't see the light at end of the tunnel, when life seemed lonesome and gloomy.

Internal cheering gives the soul a deep boost of positive energy and encouragement we can't get from others.

Cheer yourself. Cheer the little accomplishments every day, for one day, little accomplishments will be big ones.

Learn to pump yourself up. It's your approval that matters the most.

It's ok to be angry. Find out why and set it free.

There is nothing wrong with being angry with one's self, people or circumstances. It is, however, wrong to let it fester in one's being.

Try to find the root of the anger. Find your own way to heal it, forgive it, forgive you and set it free.

Brewing anger is like brewing disease in the body for free.

Ego is not your amigo.

"Check yourself before you wreck yourself," someone said.

There is nothing positive about the ego and its ability to dominate without our noticing.

Check yourself every week, or every day for that matter. Take inventory of your actions, your internal and external dialogue, and make sure that sneaky, hungry self-righteous amigo within does not take over.

Ego is ultimately fear dressed up with arrogance. Ego fools for a bit, but it eventually gets old, like the know-it-all.

Figure out where the fear comes from and find ways to heal it and empower it. It's not until then that you'll make a better amigo with yourself and others.

Friends and family.

It's said, "You are the average of the five people you associate with most."

This meaningful statement affected me deeply enough to make me take inventory of the people around me, some of whom were toxic enough to not make the cut.

Removing unhealthy associations was hard, but it ultimately allowed space for good ones ahead.

Surround yourself with good, kind, fun, smart and adventurous people who raise your game but also hold you accountable.

No one likes a whiney butt.

We all have bad days, bad circumstances and happenings, but no one like to hear sob stories over and over and over.

If you need help, ask for it because whining about it does not fix anything. It only creates more of the same, possibly escalating to worse, graduating to a victim mindset.

Turn that frown upside down. Be proactive and learn to change your verbal dialogue to what you'd like to see change.

Choose better and say it out loud.

Give and forget. Give without expectations or don't give at all.

There's nothing worse than receiving a gift later to know the gift came with an expectation, with a claim receipt.

Giving with conditions attached is worse than not giving at all.

Giving should come from the heart. It should feel organic and free of attachments. Otherwise, keep it to yourself.

Stop and smell the roses.

Literally speaking.

Life pulls us from one direction to another in seconds, making us forget to slow down and smell the roses, flowers and nature.

Stop and smell the roses, even on a foggy, smoggy day.

Slow down and take it easy. Take in the beautiful scents and beauty around you, for it might transport you exactly where your mind needed to go while finding the solutions you were looking for.

Taste with intention.

Being raised with rice, beans and tortillas can limit anyone's taste buds and their adventurous experience.

Learning to relish spices and flavors that come together to melt the heart with delicious emotions has been a gift given to myself, one I encourage you to nurture.

Honor your body by trying new foods while slowing down and thoroughly tasting any food you ingest and flavors with mindfulness and gratefulness. There is so much deliciousness to discover and many in the world who would love the luxury of food.

Relish each bite.

Listen.

This one is hard for many, including myself.

Listening is an art form.

Begin with you. Learn to listen to your body and thoughts while choosing to turn any negative thoughts to positive ones immediately. Make it a habit.

Learn to listen to your peers and strangers with great intent, and not because you want your turn to speak.

Capturing the essence in what is said and not said can reveal jewels about the person speaking.

The juice is in listening to the quiet moments when nothing is said. Yet, the silence speaks.

Move for peace.

Thank God for my cousin Beto, who instructed me to find the art in exercise when I was 11 or 12 years old, when childhood baggage began to show itself in destructive patterns and a humpy-dumpy body.

Beto showed me how to find peace and reward in jogging, stretch and movement to let off steam I didn't know was building. Movement is not only great for the mind, it's a great way to stay healthy and happy.

Find your movement in yoga, jogging, a brisk walk, weights, pilates, the options are endless. I encourage you to find a couple of modalities you like, at the very least, and walk 30-45 minutes every day. Your body deserves it; you deserve it.

Love and compliment yourself every day.

Begin and end each day with a dose of self-love and a compliment. Loving and appreciating one's self is the best compliment given. It's good for the soul; it's good for you.

Be kind. It does the body good.

It really does. Be kind to you and to others.

Faith.

Believing in a higher power, something bigger than me has been pivotal for my sanity and well-being. For me, thank God for God. I don't know what would be of me otherwise.

We can't do it on our own, with our own imperfect understanding. We need help.

Find a higher power, something bigger than you for guidance, accountability, love and comfort.

SANITY PLAYLIST

AVAILABLE ON SPOTIFY, SEARCH *"CHOOSING MAGIC"*

Gypsy ● FLEETWOOD MAC
Bleed to Love Her ● FLEETWOOD MAC
Ironic ● ALANIS MORISSETTE
Thank You ● ALANIS MORISSETTE
Hand in my Pocket ● ALANIS MORISSETTE
Walls ● TOM PETTY
Wildflowers ● TOM PETTY
Spirits ● THE STRUMBELLAS
Can't Stop the Feeling ● JUSTIN TIMBERLAKE
Stay Alive ● JOSE GONZALEZ
American Land ● BRUCE SPRINGSTEEN
Learning to Fly ● TOM PETTY
You're So Cool ● HANS ZIMMER (TRUE ROMANCE)
Now Is the Start ● A FINE FRENZY
Glory Days ● BRUCE SPRINGSTEEN
Land of Hope and Dreams ● BRUCE SPRINGSTEEN
Dancing in the Moonlight ● TOPLOADER
Don't Go Breaking my Heart ● ELTON JOHN
Landslide ● FLEETWOOD MAC
Cheek to Cheek ● ELLA FITZGERALD
Crash into Me ● DAVE MATTHEWS
Perfect Symphony ● ED SHEERAN & ANDREA BOCELLI
God Only Knows ● THE BEACH BOYS
Here Comes the Sun ● THE BEATLES
Don't You (Forget about Me) ● SIMPLE MINDS
Scenes from an Italian Restaurant ● BILLY JOEL
Summer, Highland Falls ● BILLY JOEL
One Tribe ● BLACK EYED PEAS
Born to Run ● BRUCE SPRINGSTEEN
Human Touch ● BRUCE SPRINGSTEEN
Fix You ● COLDPLAY

Just like Heaven • THE CURE
True Colors • CYNDI LAUPER
Angel Dream • TOM PETTY
I Love L.A. • RANDY NEWMAN
Father Figure • GEORGE MICHAEL
Freedom • GEORGE MICHAEL
Praying for Time • GEORGE MICHAEL
I Knew You Were Waiting for Me • GEORGE MICHAEL
& ARETHA FRANKLIN
Goodbye • THE PRETENDERS
Amazing Grace • DARLENE ZSCHECH
El Gusto • LOS LOBOS
Whenever God Shines His Light • VAN MORRISON

CHARITIES WORTH MENTIONING

RICHSTONE FAMILY CENTER

A report of child abuse is made every ten seconds, and almost five children die every day as a result of child abuse.

This praiseworthy center is dedicated to preventing and treating child abuse, strengthening families and preventing violence in families, schools and communities.

I have had the pleasure of volunteering and experiencing behind the scenes the dedication and efforts the board and staff provide to heal and change kids' broken hearts.

Please find your local center to help in the effort to heal broken hearts and prevent child abuse.

www.richstonefamily.org

HOMEBOY INDUSTRIES

A place where everyone is accepted and loved.

Homeboy Industries provides hope, training and support to formerly gang-involved and previously incarcerated men and women allowing them to direct their lives and become contributing members of our community.

I was deeply touched after interacting with and seeing the transformation that former gang-involved men and women have committed to. Change is tough. With Homeboy Industries' rehabilitation and empowering programs, homies are able to reinvent themselves in their lives and work with the love and kinship Homeboy Industries provides. It's truly remarkable to see.

www.homeboyindustries.org

ANGELS FORGOTTEN

This wonderful organization is dedicated to providing basic necessities such as food, clothing, shelter and education for children orphaned by the HIV/AIDS epidemic in Kenya.

It has been wonderful to see previously orphaned kids thrive when given the basic rights every child deserves.

www.angelsforgotten.com

ACKNOWLEDGEMENTS

This story would not be one without Amalia, my mother, whose silent tenacity, grit, hard work and resourcefulness made a way for me to have a better life in America. This book would be very different without your unapologetic force, Amalia.

Much love and appreciation to Lisa Rado, who after I doubted my written skills for many years, sternly yet kindly encouraged me to "just write it down in sections, Karina, the rest will follow." And it did. Thank you, Rado, for that simple, blunt advice and for being a great health and wellness resource for my family. Then came Jenny Linthorst, who informed me, "You now have a manuscript, Karina, you should speak with my friend to help you." Jenny, I thank you for your safe openness, support and for bringing an earthly angel along the way, Stellasue Lee, Ph.D.

Stellasue Lee, words cannot express your writing guidance, loving spirit and cheerleading as you elicited sentences I never knew were in me. You told me not to worry, to simply show up to the page, and I did. It worked, Stellasue! Thank you for your support, infectious laughter, your raw honesty and unconditional acceptance. Special thanks to my supremely talented graphic designer, Jenny Mendoza-Jenny, your ability to interpret my vision ideas into beautiful designs is beyond impressive. You are wicked talented! My editor, Linda Parsons, I appreciate you not going nuts after the many redos, additions and last-minute edits. Your promptness and professionalism are golden. Sweet Dinorah Peña Durán, you were essential in translating conversations with my mother. Muchas gracias for your time and for reminding me how beautiful our native language looks on paper. Abrazos!

My dearest friends, without you all, I'd know so much less and be so much less. Maria and David, with whom I've had some of the best conversations. Your love and deep and honest dialogue over the years have brightened and strengthened me and opened my heart. I heart you both. Utterly grateful for Milly and Mike Altieri, Bobby and Kerry Ward, Manni Morris, Starr Dangers, Ana Peters, Nicole Romero, Kristianne Thompson, Chrissie Grasso, Michelle Wattles, Kristi Buckley, Jordan and Adam Scott, Michelle Crispin, Kevin Jay Hardesty, Colleen Cole, Shan Nourian, Eli, Christine Symonds, Ana and Hugo Castillo and so many more who continue to teach me about the human spirit and the complex dance of being individuals in this thing we call life. I love how uniquely different, special and accessible you all are as you share your lives with me. Thank you for your friendship. I've grown through your lives, and sometimes your oversharing.

I've said this once, and I'll say it always...they don't make them like the Pacific brothers anymore. Although not perfect, because that would be crazy, the Pacific brothers have shown me what good men are all about with simple yet principled stances as they do their best to be good human beings, great fathers, friends and the hardest of all, husbands. Because there is an honor in it all, Jersey style. Danny, Bob, Jeff and Jerry, thank you for allowing me to write about you and your parents. You all welcomed and embraced me with open arms from day one. So happy to know each of you.

Jerry, oh my husband, The Bear. They broke the mold with you, feisty Italian Jersey boy. You keep me laughing while breaking my balls from time to time...a lot, actually. We were forced to grow up together with our very different backgrounds and cultures because God has a sense of humor, and so do we. Your eagerness to be a better man inside and out is admired by many, particularly Kyra and me. I'm proud of you. Thank you for supporting anything I've set my mind to.

My favorite human being, my Kyra girl, my superstar. You are beyond words beautiful inside and out. Thank you for being exactly who you are. The honor of being your mother is the greatest God-given gift. I love every part of you completely. Thank you for understanding my shortcomings with your innate compassion and applauding my strengths. You have taught me more than you can imagine. It has been a great ride watching you spread your wings. If I was your age, I'd want to be your friend.

Above all, I thank God. Without Your love and spirit deep in my soul, there would be no magic to choose from. You rock.

CHOOSING MAGIC
BOOK CLUB QUESTIONS

- How does the book title relate to the book's contents?

- What feelings did this book evoke for you?

- What ideas was she trying to get across?

- What questions would you ask the author?

- What aspects of the author's story could you most relate to?

- What gaps do you wish the author had filled in? Were there times that you thought she shared too much? Too little?

- Why do you think the author was motivated to tell her story?

- What have you learned after reading this book? Has it broadened your perspective about a difficult issue or topic?

- What did you like best about this book?

- Share a favorite quote or passage from the book. Why did you choose it?

- If they were making a movie of this book, who would you cast?

PRAISE FOR

CHOOSING
MAGIC

"A story of hope, Karina's beautifully etched memoir takes us along a young girl's journey from the streets of Mexico to the hills of Los Angeles, as she learns lessons big and small, everywhere finding a way to be lifted & to lift others. Karina shows us how even in the darkest of nights, "angels & heroes are placed along our path just perfectly so". This deeply personal immigration story puts a timely face to the countless families seeking to find a new identity and new life in America."
-JENNIE LINTHORST, Author of Silver Girl and Autism Disrupted: A Mother's Journey of Hope, founder of LifeSPEAKS Poetry Therapy

"This marvelous, playful, serious, sassy, enduring memoir brings joy. Karina Pacific's voice rings truth in fresh witty prose. Through sheer determination, she developed a perception for success. Her emotional quality is direct and intense. I find this work remarkably brave, a testimony to this miracle, life." **-STELLASUE LEE**, Ph. D.

"In an age when social media and filters blur reality, this story is about choosing love, forgiveness, & authenticity. Karina's journey reminds us that we are creators, not victims of our lives." **-VERA JIMENEZ**, KTLA5 Meteorologist

"What a beautiful book. Get to know my friend, Karina. You will be captivated, surprised and inspired by her story. What lessons on life and what an amazing and positive sprit she has. She is a profound observer and has a fascinating story to tell in this memoir; an incontrovertible soul living the American dream!"
-MARINA CANALS BARRERA, Actress

"In this compelling coming-of-age story, Karina beautifully describes the hardships, but also the Graces, of being raised by her single mom in Mexico, then immigrating to Los Angeles. This is a must-read for anyone yearning to understand what it is really like to overcome sexual abuse, loneliness and uncertainty to find her own strengths and power." **-PHYLLIS MITZ**, Astrologer, Author, Consultant

"Karina's book is a story about one amazing person's journey through life. This book will motivate you to examine your outlook on life. Karina's story is truly inspiring; her compassion, positive energy and caring spirt is second to none!"
-ROGER VANREMMEN, President/CEO